Protecting Judgment-Impaired Adults: Issues, Interventions and Policies

Protecting Judgment-Impaired Adults: Issues, Interventions and Policies

Edmund F. Dejowski, JD, PhD
Editor

Routledge
Taylor & Francis Group
New York London

First published 1990 by The Haworth Press, Inc.

Published 2019 by Routledge
605 Third Avenue, New York, NY 10017
2 Park Square, Milton Park, Abingdon, Oxon OX14 4RN

First issued in paperback 2021

Routledge is an imprint of the Taylor & Francis Group, an informa business

Publisher's Note
The publisher has gone to great lengths to ensure the quality of this reprint but points out that some imperfections in the original copies may be apparent.

Protecting Judgment- Impaired Adults: Issue, Interventions and Policies has also been published as Journal of Elder Abuse & Neglect, Volume 2, Numbers 3/4 1990.

Library of Congress Cataloging-in-Publication Data

Protecting judgment-impaired adults: issues, interventions, and policies / Edmund F. Dejowski, editor.
p. cm.
"Has also been published as Journal of elder abuse & neglect, volume 2, numbers 3/4, 1990" – T.p. verso.
Includes bibliographical references.
ISBN 1-56024-054-7
1. Guardian and ward – United States. 2. Capacity and disability – United States. 3. Aged – Legal status, laws, etc. – United States. 4. Aged – Care – United States. 5. Aged – Services for – United States. I. Dejowski, Edmund F.
KF553.P76 1990
344.73'0326 – dc20
[347.304326] 90-45236
CIP

ISBN 13: 978-1-138-98403-5 (pbk)
ISBN 13: 978-1-56024-054-9 (hbk)
ISBN 13: 978-1-315-82542-7 (ebk)

DOI: 10.4324/9781315825427

Protecting Judgment-Impaired Adults: Issues, Interventions and Policies

CONTENTS

ABOUT THE EDITOR

Edmund F. Dejowski, JD, PhD, a lawyer and clinical psychologist, is currently a Senior Research Associate at the Institute for Health, Health Care Policy and Aging Research, where he directs a study of the psychosocial consequences of respite care on caregivers and recipients, and several projects relating to elder abuse and money management. He was director and co-principal investigator of the Project Focus, a multi-state research and demonstration effort to identify, develop, test, and disseminate model approaches to the provision of adult protective services. This was supported by a four-year grant from the U.S. Department of Health and Human Services, contributions from the city and state of New York, and from the states of California, Maryland, and Minnesota. A major thrust of that effort was the development of improvements in laws, policies, and practices affecting judgment-impaired adults. Demonstrations included volunteer money management programs and inter-agency cooperative representative payee programs. One of the outcomes was the design of an innovative "Community Guardianship" approach to the care and protection of persons of low and moderate income. Ultimately, "Community Guardianship" was enacted into law in the state of New York. Prior to his research career, Dr. Dejowski served as Chief Psychologist of a community mental health agency.

Protecting Judgment-Impaired Adults: Issues, Interventions and Policies

Introduction

Edmund F. Dejowski, JD, PhD

The theme addressed by the contributors to this volume is guardianship and alternative methods for serving judgment-impaired adults. As a collection, their articles convey the range of disciplinary affiliations, points of view, and geographic diversity that have recently characterized this subject.

In "Evaluating Decisionmaking Capacity in the Elderly: A Review of Recent Literature," Marshall B. Kapp examines the writings appearing over the last few years on approaches to and instruments for identifying mental incapacity for legal purposes.

"Elder Abuse and Guardians of Elderly Incompetents, by Lawrence A. Frolik, advocates greater court involvement in the training and supervision of guardians. In part, Frolik proposes adding what is essentially a social service capacity to the traditional staffing pattern of probate courts. To some degree, the concept resembles the "court visitors" program that operates in Great Britain. This is an idea that deserves more discussion in the United States as well. In the endnotes, the author includes comprehensive citations to extant protective services and guardianship statutes.

The findings from four guardianship and abuse projects for the elderly which were conducted in metropolitan Chicago are described by Madelyn Anne Iris in "Uses of Guardianship as a Protective Intervention for Frail, Older Adults." From the results, it can be concluded that, even where guardianship initially appears to be an appropriate remedy, more careful analyses of client characteristics, outcomes, and available alternatives will often lead to the selection of other remedies. Interest in the study is enhanced by an extended treatment of the use of guardianships in elder abuse situations.

Bobbe Shapiro Nolan, in "A Judicial Menu: Selecting Remedies for the Incapacitated Elder," recommends a change in court law and practice such that the judge in any case involving a petition for surrogate power would have the option of shaping a remedy according to her or his perception of the need. Current law limits the court to the granting or denial of the specific relief requested in the petition. This proposal is intriguing and provocative.

Using findings from the Guardianship Diversion Project, Kathleen H. Wilber in "Material Abuse of the Elderly: When is Guardianship a Solution?" focuses on two case examples and the service decision made with respect to them. Her method of analysis provides a framework for decisionmaking that demonstrates a sensible balance: protecting the life choices made by individuals while accepting the need and appropriateness of limited guardianship under extreme and well-circumscribed conditions. This lively article provides guidance for those who must make this kind of decision on a daily basis.

"Elderly Nursing Home Residents' Need for Public Guardianship Services in Tennessee" by David Hightower, Alex Heckert, and Winsor Schmidt reports on a survey of nursing homes in Tennessee to determine the number of nursing home residents who were receiving surrogate services, including guardianship, representative payee, and power of attorney and the number of persons who might require such services. At least 1044 Tennesseans in nursing homes were identified by the homes as having an unmet need for surrogate services. Since such reports appear to be admissions against interest (i.e., the homes probably have a responsibility to refer some of these clients to public guardian programs), the numbers are likely to be underestimates. Thus, the survey constitutes strong evidence of unmet surrogate needs among judgment-impaired persons in Tennessee nursing homes.

Erich Loewy's "Social Contract, Communities and Guardians" is a theoretical treatment of guardianship which analyzes the responsibilities of the guardian from the point of view of traditional philosophies of social organization. It reflects the perspective of a discipline currently inadequately represented in the guardianship literature.

In "Managing Guardianships of the Elderly: Protection and Advocacy as Public Policy," Lloyd Hull, Gary E. Holmes, and Ronald H. Karst demonstrate how multidisciplinary personnel can work together effectively to provide guardianship to needy persons in community protection and advocacy settings. The roles of attorney, judge, assessor, and case manager are discussed with helpful, practical, and pragmatic suggestions for each of these professions.

The final selection, "Avoiding Guardianship," by George J. Alexander discusses what he perceives to be the failure of guardianship reform efforts. In response to the need for substituted judgment on behalf of incapacitated elderly persons, he proposes refocusing efforts on contractual approaches, particularly living wills and powers of attorney. Professor Alexander also explores the conflict of interest inherent in many common guardianship arrangements and analyzes the relationship of living wills to guardianships, offering a critique of new laws concerning durable powers and living wills in several states. He makes recommendations for the application of these powers to health care issues. The article is based on an address by the author to the second National Guardianship Association Conference.

OTHER DEVELOPMENTS

The array of issues and points of view presented here help the reader form some sense of the direction in which guardianship law and practice will be moving in the new decade; but notwithstanding the diverse range of viewpoints represented here, other events are also occurring that may have important effects on policy. Three elements in particular appear to have wide-ranging national implications. The first involves the development of case law concerning the scope of the guardian's authority to make decisions about the termination of life extension efforts for intractably ill individuals. The second is a proposed national guardianship act; and the third are the proposed changes in federal legislation regarding representative payees.

Role of the Individual, the Family, the Guardian, and the State in Life-Extension Decisions

For over a decade, courts in many jurisdictions have been developing case law concerning decisions to terminate treatments and services which are instrumental to life processes. The threshold questions have been whether and under what circumstances a guardian has the power to authorize the withdrawal of life support from persons in persistent vegetative states. The seminal case was In Re Quinlan, 70 N.J. 10, 355A. 2d 647 (1976), cert. denied, 429 U.S. 922, 97 S. Ct. 319 (1976). Karen Quinlan was presumed by experts to be terminally ill and in a permanent vegetative state but not "brain dead." She retained primitive reflexes such as reaction to light and pain, eye blinks, and chewing motions, and she made stereotyped cries and sounds. Her father sought guardianship for the purpose of directing that a respirator, thought essential for the continuation of the life of his daughter, be turned off. The New Jersey Supreme Court determined that the father as guardian could make the decision to disconnect the respirator if he could show that this would be her intent if she could express intent and if the decision she would have made was also objectively reasonable.

The opinion was couched in a constitutional "right to privacy" discussion, under which the court reasoned that an individual had a right to refuse medical intervention, at least under some circumstances, and that this right extended to those who could exercise it only through a guardian. In a later case the New Jersey court acknowledged that the underlying theory in the Quinlan decision had been, ". . . the individual's right to behave and act as he deems fit, provided that such behavior and activity do not conflict with the precepts of society," [In the Matter of Claire C. Conroy, 98 N.J. 321: 486 A.2d 1209 (1985)].

The Quinlan case generated much commentary and analysis; the principle that surrogates may, under certain circumstances, make decisions that treatment be terminated for comatose and chronically vegetative patients has been adopted by nearly all of the jurisdictions that have considered the issue, which encompass at least sixteen states [For a listing of over 50 cases, see Cruzan v. Harmon, 760 S.W. 2d 408 (1988)].

New Jersey and other state courts continued to expand their analysis of the power to terminate life. The major step past Quinlan was the question of decisions to terminate those interventions not conventionally thought of as medical treatment. Life-sustaining care – particularly nourishment and hydration – became the issue. In Conroy, *op.cit.*, a guardian sought to remove the gastric feeding tube which was the sole source of continuing nourishment for an elderly, incompetent nursing home resident with severe mental and physical impairments and a life expectancy of one year or less. Unlike Ms. Quinlan, Ms. Conroy was awake and conscious and able to interact with her environment to some extent. Ms. Conroy died of natural causes during the proceedings, but the court continued to hear the case. The court was especially sensitive to the fact that Ms. Conroy was in a nursing home, which made her particularly vulnerable to abuse; it found that under carefully circumscribed conditions, and after following detailed procedures laid out by the court, the guardian might make such a decision.

The Supreme Court of Missouri, to the contrary, found guardians absolutely prohibited from directing the withdrawal of nutrition or hydration. Nancy Cruzan was a thirty-year-old woman in an irreversible vegetative state from a car accident. Not long before the accident she indicated to a friend that she would not wish to have her life prolonged if she were in a vegetative state. Her family, her doctor, and a court-appointed guardian-ad-litem agreed that it was in the best interest of Ms. Cruzan for the hospital to cease the nasogastric pumping of nourishment into her body and that this would have been her wish. The trial court determined that Ms. Cruzan had a due process right to refuse continued nourishment and that this right could be asserted by her guardian under the circumstances of the case. It found by a preponderance of the evidence that Ms. Cruzan would have exercised her right to refuse treatment were she cognitively capable of doing so.

The Missouri Supreme Court reversed the decision. They based their analysis upon state law, which they said, created a strong preference for "preserving life". Unlike the other states that had grappled with similar issues, Missouri's court focused on defending the superiority of the legislature's authority to "protect the sanctity of human life" over an individual's right to self-determination or privacy. The court determined that the legislature found individuals in irreversible vegetative conditions held within them the "sanctity of human life." Because it asserted a special interest in protecting the "sanctity of human life," the legislature's claim of authority to preserve Ms. Cruzan in her current state was superior to Ms. Cruzan's claim of right to bodily self-determination or privacy, according to the court. The legislature had carved an exception to its policy, but the exception required the individual to have made a living will while competent. Because Ms. Cruzan had not executed a living will in the form prescribed by the state's legislature, the court determined that the evidence of intent was not sufficiently clear and convincing to overcome the legislatures' preference for preserving the sanctity of human life.[2]

Ms. Cruzan's parents and guardian appealed to the United States Supreme Court. Fifty-one amicus briefs were filed. Among the briefs supporting the plaintiff were those of the American Bar Association, several bioethical groups, a national association of Neurologists, the American Society of Geriatrics, and some religious denominations. Other religious organizations, States' attorneys general, and "right-to-life" organizations submitted briefs for the defendants.

A majority of the Court sustained the decision of the Missouri court [Nancy Beth Cruzan, by her Parents and Co-Guardians, Lester L. Cruzan, et Ux., Petitioners v. Director, Missouri Department of Health, et al., No. 88-1503, Supreme Court of the United States, December 6, 1989, Argued; June 25, 1990, Decided].

Critique of Cruzan

The narrow reading of the Supreme Court's opinion is that state legislatures are free to prohibit the interruption of artificial hydration and nutrition if it cannot be shown by clear and convincing evidence that the incapacitated person had a different wish. Few could object to that. However, the implications of Cruzan are much broader than these words suggest. First, the majority was not even willing to acknowledge a constitutionally-based right of competent persons to refuse interventions thought to be necessary for the extension of life. Avoiding that question, the majority were merely willing to assume "for purposes of this case," that a competent person would have a constitutionally protected right to refuse life-saving hydration and nutrition. It appears from the concurring opinion of Justice Scalia, that he, as least, would *not* have found such a right. Under these circumstances it is unknown whether the court would protect the right of individuals, even competent individuals, to decline interventions thought by a state legislature to be important to the protection or extension of their life.[3]

A second implication of Cruzan is that the state is free to establish an inflexible decision theory, as Missouri did, for determining whether to continue treatment or life support for persons unable to exercise judgment on their own behalf. Individuals who can no longer exercise judgment should have some right to ask the court, through a guardian or through their families, to have unwanted interventions discontinued. They should not be foreclosed of this right because they had never even thought about the remote contingency which has now befallen them. Despite our best efforts at education, most people will probably never consider the issue, much less convey their thoughts to others or execute a living will. That's the way life is. Such people—the majority—should not be foreclosed from the possibility of being treated as would wish, not as the legislature has determined. But no relief would be available to them under Missouri's approach regardless of particular circumstances. After Cruzan, the family has no recourse against states that impose policies which make relief a practical impossibility for most persons.

Third, the court heard Missouri's defense, which everyone seemed to agree was rooted in the state's asserted interest in preserving the sanctity of human life. But the court's majority failed to question Missouri's basis or authority for legislatively determining when a body is endowed with, or loses, "the sanctity of human life." Missouri determined that permanently vegetative and insensate human corpora are endowed with it. Such a view is consistent with some religious traditions, but is also strongly at odds with many other long-established faiths, such as those which define the essence of being human with reference to the exercise of thought, reason, and judgment.

Death is a pragmatic determination that must be made to protect the health of the community. Under certain easy-to-specify circumstances a body will begin to putrefy. At that point its removal and disposal become imperative. The state need not address questions of whether the body still possesses a special metaphysical essence to make a determination of death. Ms. Cruzan's body may not be dead. But what Missouri does is to determine by legislation that Ms Cruzan retains the spiritual essence that many believe makes homo sapiens human, that which imparts to this life-form the sanctity ascribed to it by the Missouri legislature. That is quite different from stating that she is not dead. So long as Missouri's legislators offer even a thin rational pretext, the United States Supreme Court's majority says the Constitution leaves Missouri's elected officials free to tell Missourians when the human spirit is and when it is not present in their body. Surely, if the framers of the Constitution meant to offer individuals any protection against the state, they must have meant to protect them at least from this. The issue is of vital significance to the abortion debate. If the state can determine when a body is sanctified with the spirit of human life, it is constitutionally free to prohibit or restrict abortions, relying on its "interest in protecting human life" to outbalance the female's interest in bodily privacy and self-determination. It would be difficult to avoid noting in this connection that Missouri was, at the time of the Cruzan case, defending its landmark anti-abortion law, which had been sustained by the State's Supreme Court (Webster v. Reproductive Services, 492 U.S.______,1989). It seems likely that other states will now be tempted to join Missouri in using the issue in their ideological battles concerning abortion.

Finally, the simplest human terms, the Court had the opportunity to use its wisdom and authority to ameliorate the plight of Nancy Cruzan and her family. Instead, the majority dealt with the issue in the narrowest and most ideological way. The intelligent men and woman of the majority surely recognized that the Cruzan family had become a piece on a wider game board. Neither the Cruzans nor the many other families raked by similar tragedies are likely to benefit much from this Court's action.

National Standards and the Right to a Guardian

In 1988 and again in 1989 a bill promoted by the late Representative Claude Pepper has been introduced into both Houses of Congress. Entitled the National Guardianship Rights Act (S 235 and H 1706, 101st Cong.), it would require states to adopt a range of standards for guardianship in order to continue to receive certain federal funds. Among its major provisions are requirements that states modify guardianship proceedings to provide certain protections, including a right to a guardian if the need is established. Guardians would be required to report to the court at least annually on the financial, mental, physical, and personal status of the incapacitated person, and courts would be required to provide continuing oversight at least annually by investigating the well-being of persons under their orders of guardianship. The order must be dissolved if and when the need ceases.

Procedural protections established in the bill include a nonwaivable right of prompt notice to allegedly incapacitated individuals; a right to be present at all proceedings, unless disability prevents attendance; a right to counsel; and a right to an independent professional guardianship evaluation team of specified membership to examine the individual, report, and be available for questioning; a right to dismissal of the guardianship action if the team determines the individual to be free of any incapacity; a right to a jury; a right to present evidence, call witnesses, and cross examine; and a right to prompt appeal. The bill establishes a minimum standard for establishing a guardianship: clear and convincing evidence of incapacity and a finding that no less restrictive form of intervention is available. It prohibits use of advanced age alone as a basis for determining incapacity, limits the scope and duration of the guardian's responsibility, and reserves to the incapacitated individual all rights not expressly transferred in the guardianship order.

States must submit implementation plans to the Attorney General of the United States indicating compliance. Federal grants are authorized to promote compliance, and mandatory sanctions are to be imposed on states that do not comply.

The bill did not pass in the 101st Congress. Enactment of the legislation would assure a rather enlightened minimum standard for guardianship across the nation. The aspect of the legislation that might have the greatest ultimate impact is the duty it appears to impose on the state judiciary to secure competent guardianship services for all persons who are found to need it. Because of the ubiquitous unavailability of guardians for persons of low and moderate income, an implication of this requirement is that pressure would build for the establishment of guardianship services in many states. Although the list of sponsors has grown from the time of the bill's initial introduction, the death of Claude Pepper, who was the primary force in moving the bill, places its fate in jeopardy. Furthermore, the American Bar Association, which endorses guardianship recommendations very similar to many of the provisions in the bill and which might have been expected to offer strong support, has refused to take a position on it.

One of the reasons for this apparent paradox appears to be that within the American Bar Association's Section of Real Property, Probate and Trust Law, a committee concerned with the problems of guardians opposes federal reform: the bill could have substantial impact on the practices of attorneys who serve as guardians or conservators. This important legislation would have a profound impact on guardianship nationally, but unless a strong Congressional advocate takes up the cause, it is unlikely to move forward. (Claude Pepper's analysis of the bill and his assessment of the need for it appears in *The Journal of Elder Abuse & Neglect*, *1*(3), 1989).

Avoiding Guardianship with Representative Payees

Also having important implications for the future course of guardianship is a proposal to permit certain non-profit agencies to collect fees for representative payee services. At the present time, the law does not address compensation for the costs incurred in providing representative payee services to Social Security or Supplemental Security Income recipients. Social Security Administration (SSA) regulations permit a representative payee to deduct from the beneficiary's monthly check only the actual out-of-pocket expenses of providing payee services, such as stamps, travel, and phone expenses.

The SSA once permitted certain organizations providing representative payee services to collect a fee for services from the beneficiary's check, but, citing a lack of statutory authority, it discontinued this practice. As a result, it is necessary for agencies to seek guardianships so that the court can direct compensation from the estate, even in cases where representative payee status alone would have been sufficient to meet the needs of the incapacitated individual.

Amendments were proposed in the House of Representatives to modify the Social Security Act so that community-based nonprofit social service agencies (defined as agencies that are representative of communities or significant segments of communities and regularly provide services to those in need) serving as payee for more than five recipients would have been able to draw a fee to cover direct costs and overhead from the benefits they administer for serving as representative payee (135 Cong. rec. 5984, September 27, 1989). However, these provisions were dropped in committee (Conference Report on H.R. 3299, 135 Cong. Rec. H 9333, November 21, 1989).

Some 550,000 individuals have representative payees. Many commentators have opined that the representative payee option provides an opportunity to put needed services in place early and quickly, allowing the payee to pay neglected bills and make necessary purchases so that an individual who is declining physically or mentally never reaches the state of extreme physical and environmental neglect when guardianship or long-term institutional care becomes the only viable option. The lack of funding sources through which agencies might support payee programs has prevented any serious test of this theory. It is unfortunate that the proposal has made so little headway. However, the momentum for reform in this area is strong, and if funding is made available for agencies to conduct representative payee services, a considerable decline might be noted in the number of low-income guardianships that are being sought.

Need for Evaluation

The papers presented here, the emerging case law, and the proposed national reforms discussed above, demonstrate the quality and richness of thinking on the subject of guardianship. Unfortunately scientifically valid data on the extent and nature of the need, on the current status of guardianship across the country, and on the relative effectiveness of different approaches, are almost unavailable. Much of contemporary guardianship policy has developed by "muddling through." Too often changes in guardianship laws and practices have been politically motivated reactions to revelations of harm to an incapacitated individual. Changes wrought under such circumstances are not likely to be careful and well-reasoned. Further, the momentum for reform is often lost as soon as a change has been implemented. Unsatisfactory results from ill-conceived reforms may lead to an unwillingness to take further risks and to create new solutions. The challenge for the nineties is the orderly implementation and *testing* of well-reasoned reform proposals. These efforts should always be accompanied by independent, controlled, scientifically valid evaluations of the outcome. Changes in policy and practice should be regarded as tentative and experimental until such findings are reported.

I would like to thank Rosalie S. Wolf and Susan McMurray Anderson, co-editors of the *Journal of Elder Abuse & Neglect*, for suggesting the theme and providing invaluable technical assistance and helpful advice in all aspects of the development of this work.

NOTES

1. The statute in any event did not recognize the power to direct the withholding of hydration or nutrition through living wills (Mo. Rev. Stat. §459.010 et seq. (1986)).

2. According to Justice Stevens, dissenting in Cruzan, "The clear and convincing standard of proof has been variously defined in this context as 'proof sufficient to persuade the trier of fact that the patient held a firm and settled commitment to the termination of life supports under the circumstances like those presented,' In re Westchester County Medical Center on behalf of O'Connor, 72 N. Y. 2d 517, 531, N. E. 2d 607, 613 (1988) (O'Connor), and as evidence which 'produces in the mind of the trier of fact a firm belief or conviction as to the truth

of the allegations sought to be established, evidence so clear, direct and weighty and convincing as to enable [the factfinder] to come to a clear conviction, without hesitancy, of the truth of the precise facts in issue,' In re Jobes, 108 N. J., at 407-408, 529 A. 2d, at 441 (quotation omitted)."

3. That the court, as presently constituted, reached such a result is not suprising. Its majority has not been a defender of individual privacy against state action, even in the most personal aspects of human living (see, e.g., Bowers v. Hardwick, 478 U.S. 186, holding state free to criminalize sexual acts between consenting adults performed in private, even though state unable to show compelling rationale).

Evaluating Decisionmaking Capacity in the Elderly: A Review of Recent Literature

Marshall B. Kapp, JD, MPH

SUMMARY. This article critically reviews and analyzes recent contributions to the medical and legal literature dealing with the subject of defining and assessing decisionmaking capacity in older patients/clients. The themes and issues set forth in this burgeoning literature are described and guidelines are commented upon in terms of their usefulness to practitioners and the ethical and social policy implications they raise.

INTRODUCTION

Before a proxy decisionmaker in the form of a guardian or conservator may be appointed by a court to act on behalf of an individual, the court must make a determination that the individual in question (the ward) presently lacks the mental capacity to make decisions on his[1] own behalf. There is widespread acceptance of the concept that, because of primary mental illness or physical maladies with medical or psychological consequences, some people are not able to understand and appreciate the quality of their decisions and to engage in an autonomous, authentic decisionmaking process (Tremblay, 1987). However, the attempt to achieve a precise, easily measurable and applied legal definition of decisional incapacity

Marshall B. Kapp is Professor in the Department of Medicine in Society at Wright State University School of Medicine, Box 927, Dayton, OH 45401-0927, and also serves as Adjunct Professor at the University of Dayton School of Law.

1. For the sake of simplicity, the masculine pronoun is used throughout this article.

was likened over a decade ago to a "search for the Holy Grail" (Roth, Meisel & Lidz, 1977). Little has happened in the realm of statutory or case law development in the recent past to change that assessment. Although standards differ slightly among the jurisdictions, legislatures and courts continue to define decisional capacity, if at all, only broadly and vaguely. To the consternation of health care, human service, and legal professionals who work with older persons of questionable capacity, the mechanical "competency meter" to which an individual might be connected and a numerical "readout" produced has not yet been invented.

Nonetheless, voluminous literature in the health, human service, and (to a much lesser extent) in legal journals has arisen in the subject area of defining and assessing decisional capacity, particularly for the elderly for whom memory, intelligence, and problem-solving ability may be compromised. Especially in the absence of precise guidelines provided by legal authorities, this literature is significant, for it informs actions by those professionals whose judgments about patient[2] decisional capacity (as will be discussed further below) generally *de facto* determine whether the individual's spoken choice will be followed or formal or informal proxy decisionmaking will occur. This article identifies some common threads or issues discussed in a few recent selections from this burgeoning literature.

COMMON THEMES

Criteria or Tests of Capacity

There is widespread acceptance by now of the concept that decisional capacity is a matter of the patient's functional ability to make decisions, rather than one that is automatically determined by agreement or disagreement with an outcome (that is, whether or not the decision itself is one that a 'reasonable' person would have reached) or the patient's status or membership in a particular 'vul-

---

2. The term "patient" is used in this article to describe the person whose decisional capacity is in doubt, although "client" or "consumer" might also be an appropriate description.

nerable' class based on age or medical diagnosis. "The most important task for the legal standard of competency is to distinguish effectively between foolish, socially deviant, risky, or simply 'crazy' choices made competently, and comparable choices made incompetently. Although incompetent behavior may be restrained, identical competent behavior may not" (Tremblay, 1987).

Under the heading of functional assessment for decisionmaking purposes, four distinct but related standards are mentioned repeatedly (Appelbaum & Grisso, 1988; Stanley, Stanley, Guido & Garvin, 1988). First, is the patient able to evidence and communicate a choice, and one that is stable enough over time to permit its effectuation? Second, can the patient understand relevant information, both in terms of specific facts and the patient's own role in the decisionmaking process? This standard has the virtue of relatively easy testability, but depends heavily on the patient's verbal (rather than reasoning) skills. Third, what is the quality of the patient's thinking process; can the patient manipulate information logically? Is the patient able to weigh the decisional factors according to the values that the patient himself has assigned those factors? Is the outcome of the patient's decisionmaking exercise consistent with his starting premises? Fourth, does the patient appreciate the nature of his own situation (e.g., rather than denying a serious medical problem or risk) and the consequences of the decision for himself?

In a pragmatic roadmap to capacity assessment in the context of refusal of antipsychotic medications by a mentally disordered patient, one psychiatrist (Beck, 1987) has broken these criteria down into two elements: (1) capacity to assimilate relevant facts and (2) appreciation or rational understanding of the patient's situation as it relates to the facts. Beck's clinical definition that combines these two elements states that a mentally disordered person has capacity to refuse treatment if he is aware of having a mental disorder, has sufficient factual knowledge about medication and mental disorder, and does not base refusal on delusional beliefs.

Broken down further, Beck's criterion of capacity for assimilating relevant facts requires that the patient be educated about, and aware of, pertinent facts but not that the patient agree with the clinician's interpretation of those facts. Put differently, the patient who says in effect, "I know what you say, but I do not agree," possesses decisional capacity.

Beck reduces the rational understanding criterion to two parts. Under the heading "Acknowledgement versus Denial of Illness," he states that a patient may deny his illness either correctly, because in fact there is no illness, or incorrectly because the patient does not understand his own situation. Only denial of a real illness signals decisional incapacity; consequently, the clinician's first task in this formulation is to verify the existence of an actual illness that the patient is denying. Under the heading "Delusional Basis for Refusal," Beck declares that delusions only produce decisional incapacity if they relate to the treatment refusal. The clinician should probe whether even the delusional patient's choice rests on some other, realistic foundation.

The distinction between comprehension of facts, on one hand, and the quality of reasoning using those facts, on the other, as separate elements of decisional capacity is illustrated in recent research by Stanley et al., (1988). In their study, this team compared the capacity of patients with mild or moderate Alzheimer's disease to that of older persons with major depression, to determine whether these groups encounter special problems with the informed consent process beyond those difficulties that have been identified previously in the general elderly population. Based on individual interviews with the subjects during which quantitative measurements were assigned, these researchers found no differences with respect to quality of reasoning between the cognitively impaired, the depressed, and a control group. Even the cognitively impaired could weigh risks and benefits, at least globally. However, this study found significant differences in the comprehension of consent information, with the Alzheimer's patients experiencing the most difficulty. Stanley et al., posit even greater problems for the more severely cognitively impaired.

Psychiatrists Gutheil and Bursztajn (1986) emphasize that decisional capacity depends not just on cognitive factors, but can also be influenced by psychotic states and affective disorders. They submit that many physicians, attorneys, judges, and guardians *ad litem* are 'taken in' by incapacitated individuals who successfully feign decisional ability through their talent for remembering and reciting information without understanding or appreciating its meaning for them. Typical patient types in this category are the 'glib paranoid,' the pessimistic and severely depressed patient, the denying manic or hypomanic person, or the patient with anorexia nervosa.

Lawrence Hipshman (1987) proposes a new model for assessing decisional capacity: the patient's ability to form a workable 'therapeutic alliance' with the clinician. Under what he calls the 'legal' component of his model, he would inquire whether the patient is able to consult effectively with the clinician regarding treatment (an inquiry intentionally analogous to the Supreme Court's *Dusky* (1960) standard of ability to consult with and assist legal counsel as the determinant of a criminal defendant's competency to stand trial). Taken by itself, Lipshman's therapeutic alliance definition of capacity seems to beg the question; it is precisely the issue of the patient's ability to work 'effectively' with the clinician that is at stake. However, Hipshman's so-called 'ethical' or autonomy component defines 'effective' decisionmaking in a manner that makes his model potentially quite useful: Does the patient, collaborating with the clinician, have the capacity to express his own beliefs and preferences and to make decisions consistent with those personal values? In other words, are the patient's choices authentic for him? Importantly, if the impediment to the formation of an effective therapeutic alliance stems from some factor other than the patient's cognitive or psychological deficits (such as a personality rift between patient and clinician), decisional incapacity should not be inferred.

Limits of Standardized Tests

A number of standardized tests for measuring mental functioning in the elderly have been developed (Grisso, 1986). Silver (1987) and Baker (1989) are among recent authors who have reviewed screening tests of cognitive ability frequently used with the elderly in clinical practice. The former described the Alzheimer's Disease Assessment Scale, Weschler Adult Intelligence Scale, and the Weschler Memory Scale. Psychiatrist Baker compares the Folstein Mini-Mental State Examination, Kahn Mental Status Questionnaire, Cognitive Capacity Screening Examination, Mattis Dementia Rating Scale, and Kokmen Short Test of Mental Status. While Dr.

Baker cites standardization and quick administerability by nurses as benefits of these tests, it is admitted that they are preliminary screening instruments only (i.e., first steps), rather than the final word on a patient's capacity, and that the choice of instrument ought to vary depending on what aspect of the patient's mentation is being measured: orientation, memory, cognitive processing, or neurologic functioning.

Other current literature highlights the limitations of bedside mental status examinations and standardized screening devices by themselves to assess decisional capacity (Farnsworth, 1989; Hipshman, 1987). Naugle and Kawczak (1989) note that one of the most commonly employed screening devices, the Mini-Mental State Examination, is intended for use for diagnostic—hence, treatment—purposes. Even so restricted, problems with false positives and false negatives in identifying cognitive impairment abound. Although this instrument was in no way devised for use in assessing decisional capacity, it is frequently misused by clinicians for that purpose.

On the other hand, physician Gerald Goodenough (1988) argues the virtues, in terms of improved objectivity of physician evaluations of mental capacity, of using a standardized functional testing instrument and recording findings on a uniform form. He decries the fact that, in assessing mental capacity in a guardianship context, there are no objective criteria as there are for most other phenomena (such as the existence of a physical disability in the Workers' Compensation context) that the physician is asked to evaluate. He criticizes most physician reports on decisional capacity as conclusory, based on diagnosis (i.e., the patient's status) rather than a determination of how, if at all, that diagnosis affects the patient's ability to function. Among the problems Goodenough refers to in physician evaluations are medical bias against the elderly and toward the family seeking control, a failure to realize that capacity may be a transient state, undue influence of communication problems in the older patient, and a general misunderstanding of the reason for a capacity evaluation.

While favoring the spread of standard functional testing instruments and recording forms to improve objectivity, Goodenough expresses pessimism that the average practicing physician has the financial or professional incentive to learn better techniques for such medicolegal assessments. In addition, he ignores the probability that widespread use of standard devices for assessing decisional capacity would encourage physician overreliance, resulting in a mechanical filling-in-the-blanks thinking process de-emphasizing appropriate professional judgment and flexibility.

Decision-Specific Nature of Capacity: Sliding Scale Standard

It is by now uniformly accepted in the literature (even if not yet universally applied in medical or legal practice) that capacity to make personal choices must be judged on a decision-specific, as opposed to a global or all-or-nothing, basis. A patient's capacity must be judged according to the particular decision with which that patient is confronted, whether medical, legal (e.g., conducting a certain business transaction) (Smith, 1988), or other in nature. A patient may be generally capable of making most decisions but unable emotionally (Gutheil, Bursztajn, Kaplan & Brodsky, 1987) to weigh risks and benefits concerning a specific question, or not able to comprehend information or engage in a rational thought process on most matters but capable of focusing sufficiently on a specific matter of importance to him (Farnsworth, 1989; Mahler & Perry, 1988). In a similar vein, there is broad consensus in the literature that capacity may be partial or compromised rather than entirely absent. Capacity thus may fall or fluctuate along points of a continuum, instead of resting at either end (Kloezen, Fitten & Steinberg, 1988). Likewise, there is little dispute that decisional capacity refers only to a minimal or baseline functional level, rather than an ideal of perfect comprehension and rational thought (Appelbaum & Grisso, 1988).

Since mental capacity is decision-specific and fluctuates along a continuum, some have proposed that it be evaluated according to a sliding scale, where less capacity is required for questions that are simpler or carry less serious consequences than for more complex or consequential decisions (Drane, 1984; Drane, 1985; President's Commission, 1982). Although courts have not explicitly adopted this concept, Appelbaum and Grisso (1988) surmise that judicial findings may be affected implicitly by the potential consequences of the decision facing the patient at the time of inquiry.

Many commentators reject the notion of a sliding scale, arguing that the assessor should not adjust the standard of capacity required but instead ought to apply an unchanging standard of capacity to the particular decision in question. Thus, the standard of capacity remains constant but its application depends on the specific case—both in terms of the unique patient and the unique choice encountered. For example, Kloezen et al., (1988) would replace a sliding scale of decisional capacity approach with the use of a combination of increasingly complex hypothetical clinical vignettes, where the patient's answers are scored against 'normal' responses, and a uniform mental status examination. Mahler and Perry (1988) reject the sliding scale idea in favor of a three-step process: (1) focusing on the capacity to make specific decisions and placing the patient's ability on a spectrum of impairment; (2) using the Hundert (1987) method of identifying and weighing all conflicting values in the case, while recognizing the law's presumption of patient autonomy; and (3) working with the patient and staff to reach a mutual decision, while keeping open the possibility of judicial involvement.

Assisted Decisional Capacity: Information, Treatment, Manipulating the Environment

Consistent with the concept of decisional capacity being of a choice-specific, spectrum nature rather than falling in an all-or-nothing category, commentators universally endorse the notion of 'assisted capacity.' This doctrine holds that many older persons, although perhaps not capable of making entirely autonomous, authentic decisions completely on their own, are nonetheless able to muster 'enough' powers of comprehension and rational thinking when given the proper degree of assistance, encouragement, and support by others. This assistance to render the older person sufficiently able to function as decisionmaker may take the form of providing adequate information, treating underlying medical problems, and manipulating environmental factors.

Family physician Farnsworth (1989) underscores that what appears as incompetent treatment refusal by an elderly patient often is a matter of the patient being inadequately informed about the nature, rationale, and projected benefits of the proposed medical intervention. Appelbaum and Grisso (1988) caution that the capacity evaluator cannot assume that the patient has been informed adequately. Farnsworth suggests that third party mediation occasionally may be worthwhile in this regard. A study by Beck of state mental hospital inpatients and antipsychotic medications (Beck, 1988) concluded that apparent decisional incapacity can be corrected for many patients by providing them with more pertinent information (i.e., improving their factual knowledge), to go along with their rational understanding. Continual education of the patient concerning benefits and risks of treatment, according to Beck, not only improves decisional capacity, but makes rational consent and compliance more likely.

Tymchuk et al., (1988) discovered that the manner in which information is presented to elderly persons substantially affects comprehension. In their study, consent information given to older nursing home patients (all of whom were pre-judged by facility staff to be mentally capable) in simplified and storybook formats was understood better than information presented in a standard format. The study also found that older persons faced with important decisions want, and are able to handle, substantial amounts of information. Results provide some support for the hypothesis that a simplified or storybook presentation of information format improves quality of reasoning as well as factual comprehension. Tymchuk et al., recommend, in addition to simplification of the subject matter for the patient, that the information so simplified ought to be presented in repeated immediate (massed practice) or repeated delayed (distributed practice) fashion to reinforce the message.

Evaluation of decisional incapacity may also be confounded by the presence of a treatable underlying medical pathology. The primary precept of Gutheil and Bursztajn's credo (1986) is to intervene clinically first. Appelbaum and Grisso (1988) urge that the patient be given a chance to exhibit his highest level of mental functioning and that treating medically treatable conditions initially may often improve that functional level and thereby enhance the patient's autonomy. Mahler and Perry (1988) also stress the clinician's early duty to recognize and minister to non-cognitive problems like interpersonal patient/staff barriers, depression, delirium, or denial that may interfere with the patient's capacity and undergird his treatment refusal. For all of these authors, the clinician's duty to explore, rule out, or intervene regarding underlying medical problems precedes any resort to the courts for the involuntary imposition of a substitute decisionmaker. To illustrate the clinician's role in investigating the possible physical bases for a patient's seemingly irrational decision, Kloezen et al., (1988) describe a case where, once the patient's family convinced him to take his blood pressure medicine, the patient's capacity improved markedly.

Besides admonishing clinicians to make certain that the patient has been properly informed and that treatable physical conditions have been addressed, the literature is also clear that clinicians should account for environmental factors in assessing capacity and should manipulate those factors where appropriate. Since capacity often varies over time and according to physical surroundings (Farnsworth, 1989), clinicians are advised to rely on multiple examinations conducted over a period of time and, ideally, in a variety of settings (Appelbaum & Grisso, 1988). An attempt to rehabilitate a seemingly cognitively compromised patient to make the best use of his existing capacity (Kloezen et al., 1988) also entails taking into account, and responding to through education of both patient and evaluator, special ethnic, cultural, and educational factors manifesting themselves as barriers to decisional capacity (Appelbaum & Grisso, 1988).

The value of family, friends, and professional caregivers in assisting the patient to deal more competently with difficult decisions through general support and encouragement is a constant thread in the literature. As Gutheil et al., (1987) explain, a person who is bolstered by supportive relationships (including the therapeutic alliance with a medical professional) may be better able to cope with tough choices than one who feels all alone and consequently is overwhelmed by anxiety. Evaluation of capacity is an ongoing process influenced integrally by patient interactions with others (Mahler & Perry, 1988).

Capacity versus Competence: Clinical Assessment versus Judicial Intervention

The literature in both medicine and law today draws a sharp distinction between the concepts of decisional capacity, on one hand, and competency, on the other. The former term relates to the opinion of a clinical evaluator concerning an individual's functional ability to make autonomous, authentic decisions about his own life. The latter term refers to the judgment of a court of law about the same issue, which generally is the prelude to appointment of a proxy decisionmaker over the objection, or at least without the voluntary consent, of the person deemed to be incompetent. The clinician only opines whether the patient 'appears' to have capacity to make a particular decision within a specific social/medical context, but does not possess the authority to ultimately decide if the patient is legally competent (Mahler & Perry, 1988).

There is strong support for the "least restrictive alternative" position (Kloezen et al., 1988) that most cases involving decisionmaking for persons of questionable functional status are better dealt with through evaluation of capacity rather than competence. That is, resort to the courts to resolve the issue, with the resultant creation of a guardianship or conservatorship, should be avoided wherever possible (Annas & Densberger, 1984).

Commentators agree that it is the treating clinician's role in the first instance to gather data and to decide whether the particular circumstances trigger the need to seek (1) further clinical consultation regarding the patient's capacity and/or (2) a judicial adjudication of incompetence and formal appointment of a surrogate (Appelbaum & Grisso, 1988). There are no clear guidelines on this largely ethical question of when the presumption of competence has been sufficiently rebutted and the circumstances as a whole compel resort to the courts (Hipshman, 1987).

One geriatrician (Stollerman, 1989) asserts that an appraisal of mental capacity should occur at the outset of every encounter with an older patient (or any age patient, for that matter), at least implicitly. Stollerman laments that usually such appraisal is completely omitted from the medical record. His own appraisal guidelines are described by the acronym ROAMS: Reaction, Orientation, Affect, Memory, and Speech.

When the treating clinician is an attorney—that is, when the issue of mental capacity arises in the context of a client of questionable mental capacity relating to an attorney for the purpose of obtaining legal services—that clinician too must make an initial assessment of the patient/client's ability to make autonomous, authentic decisions, in this case regarding the exercise of legal (rather than medical) options. The American Bar Association's 1969 Model Code of Professional Responsibility and 1983 Model Rules of Professional Conduct fail to provide any guidance to the attorney for assessing a person's functional capacity, beyond a permission (not a mandate) to consult an unspecified 'diagnostician.'

Attorney Linda Smith (1988) suggests that consultation with medical diagnosticians may be useful to the attorney in documenting the patient's capacity in case the issue is raised later and in facilitating the attorney's attempt to assist (Smith calls it 'gradual counseling') the somewhat compromised patient in a decisionmaking process that obviates the need for court intervention. At the same time, she suggests caution because invoking a medical diagnostician may upset the patient/client and because many clinicians return assessments concentrating on medical diagnosis rather than functional evaluation and on global rather than decision-specific capacity. For Smith, the attorney's key threshhold concern is determining when, based upon the attorney's own preliminary assessment, further clinical or judicial involvement is unavoidable, as opposed to relying on 'gradual counseling' and collaboration with informal proxy decisionmakers to achieve the patient/client's best interests or substituted judgment.

When cases are brought into the judicial arena, there is consensus that judges' determinations of legal competence are very heavily influenced by clinical opinions concerning capacity (Mahler & Perry, 1988), to the point where courts in large measure have 'turfed' the problem of mental capacity to the clinicians (where the majority of commentators argue that the issue properly belongs) (Hipshman, 1987). Vital in this aspect of forensic medicine—the application of medical expertise and experience to help resolve legal issues—are the clinician's notes in the patient's record (Farnsworth, 1989). Gutheil and Bursztajn (1986) counsel their psychiatric colleagues to anticipate the possibility that a patient's mental capacity may become an issue, and to document thoroughly the clinical determinants (i.e., the facts) supporting the clinician's view regarding capacity or incapacity. Consultations concerning the patient's capacity with family, treatment and forensic specialists, and other professional staff who have contact with the patient also should be documented in the patient's chart.

Leading forensic psychiatrists and psychologists emphasize the value of clinician (especially psychiatrist/attorney collaboration on difficult capacity assessment cases (Appelbaum & Grisso, 1988). For Gutheil et al., (1987), the attorney as an advocate focusing on short-term rights and the clinician as an expert investigator and therapist concentrating on long-term benefits make a powerful and constructive team. Moreover, the clinician has an essential role in educating institutional attorneys and the courts about clinical issues and in employing attorneys in the presentation of clinically probative evidence (Gutheil & Bursztajn, 1986).

CONCLUSION

A legally and clinically usable definition of decisional competence that is both sufficiently specific to avoid false positives and broad enough to avoid false negatives is probably impossible; some clinical and judicial leeway is both inevitable and desirable (Mahler & Perry, 1988). Moreover, a determination of clinical capacity or legal competence does answer the more important question of what particular choice ought to be made by or for the patient. Nonetheless, the assessment of capacity is a vital threshhold issue for those concerned about decisionmaking by and for older persons, the extent of individual autonomy versus protectionism, and the implications of substitute decisionmaker involvement. The type of medical and legal literature reviewed in this article will continue to grow, based on clinical experience, empirical investigation, and philosophical and legal analysis, as commentators continue to identify and flesh out the common threads discussed above.

REFERENCES

Appelbaum, P.S. & Grisso, T. (1988). Assessing patients' capacity to consent to treatment. *New England Journal of Medicine, 319*(25), 1635-38.

Annas, G.J. & Densberger, J. (1984). Competence to refuse medical treatment: autonomy vs. paternalism. *University of Toledo Law Review, 15*, 561-596.

Baker, F.M. (1989). Screening tests for cognitive impairment. *Hospital and Community Psychiatry, 40*, 339-340.

Beck, J.C. (1987). Right to refuse antipsychotic medication: Psychiatric assessment and legal decisionmaking. *Mental and Physical Disability Law Reporter, 11*, 368-372.

Beck, J.C. (1988). Determining competency to assent to neuroleptic drug treatment. *Hospital and Community Psychiatry, 39*, 1106-1108.

Drane, J.F. (1984). Competency to give informed consent. *Journal of the American Medical Association, 252*, 925-927.

Drane, J.F. (1985). The many faces of competency. *Hastings Center Report, 15*, 17-21.

Dusky v. *United States*, 362 U.S. 402, 80 Sup. Ct. 788 (1960).

Farnsworth, M.G. (1989). Evaluation of mental competency. *American Family Physician, 39*, 182-190.

Goodenough, G.K. (1988). The lack of objectivity of physician evaluations in geriatric guardianship cases. *Journal of Contemporary Law, 14*, 53-59.

Grisso, T. (1986). *Evaluating competencies: Forensic assessments and instruments*. New York: Plenum Press.

Gutheil, T.G. & Bursztajn, H. (1986). Clinicians' guidelines for assessing and presenting subtle forms of patient incompetence in legal settings. *American Journal of Psychiatry, 143*, 1020-1023.

Gutheil, T.G., Bursztajn, H., Kaplan, A.N. & Brodsky, A. (1987). Participation in competency assessment and treatment decisions: The role of a psychiatrist-attorney team. *Mental and Physical Disability Law Reporter, 11*, 446-449.

Hipshman, L. Defining a clinically useful model for assessing competence to consent to treatment. *Bulletin of the American Academy of Psychiatry and Law, 15*, 235-245.

Hundert, E.M. (1987). A model for ethical problem solving in medicine, with practical applications. *American Journal of Psychiatry, 144*, 839-846.

Kloezen, S., Fitten, L.J. & Steinberg, A. (1988). Assessment of treatment decision-making capacity in a medically ill patient. *Journal of the American Geriatrics Society, 36*, 1055-1058.

Mahler, J. & Perry, S. (1988). Assessing competency in the physically ill: guidelines for psychiatric consultants. *Hospital and Community Psychiatry, 39*, 856-861.

Naugle, R.I. & Kawczak, K. (1989). Limitations of the Mini-Mental State Examination. *Cleveland Clinic Journal of Medicine, 56*, 277-281.

President's Commission for the Study of Ethical Problems in Medicine and

Biomedical and Behavioral Research. (1982). *Making health care decisions, vol. 1*. Washington, D.C.

Roth, L.H., Meisel, A. & Lidz, C. (1977). Tests of competency to consent to treatment. *American Journal of Psychiatry, 134*, 279-283.

Silver, H.M. (1987). Alzheimer's disease: ethical and legal decisions. *Medicine and Law, 6*, 537-551.

Smith, L.F. (1988). Representing the elderly client and addressing the question of competence. *Journal of Contemporary Law, 14*, 61-104.

Stollerman, G.H. (1989). Assessment of the person. *Hospital Practice*, April 30, 13-17.

Tremblay, P.R. (1987). On persuasion and paternalism: Lawyer decisionmaking and the questionably competent client. *Utah Law Review, 3*, 515-584.

Tymchuk, A.J., Ouslander, J.G., Rahbar, B. & Fitten, J. (1988). Medical decision-making among elderly people in long term care. *Gerontologist, 28* (Special Supplement), 59-63.

Elder Abuse and Guardians of Elderly Incompetents

Lawrence A. Frolik, JD

SUMMARY. Caregivers vary widely in their behavior toward those for whom they care. Some are very good while others cross over into criminal behavior. Guardians, as one category of caregivers, undoubtedly parallel other caregivers in their behavior patterns in that behavior stretches from the very good to the criminal. The courts who appoint guardians have the responsibility to see that guardians do not abuse or neglect their wards. For courts to improve the performance of guardians will require that the courts have an effective system of accountability by the guardians as to how they have performed and the power to fine or otherwise penalize errant guardians. Finally, the courts must be given the resources necessary to perform the review function. The court must be transformed from a passive to a proactive entity and be supplied with the staff required to adequately supervise the guardians that it appoints.

INTRODUCTION

Care and neglect, love and abuse, white and black: who is to say where one begins and the other leaves off. White turns to gray and then to black, but at what point? Love turns cold and the coolness of indifference turns to abuse. At the extremes, abuse and neglect are clear and visible. But in the middle, in the area between abuse and love, and neglect and care, appear scores of "gray" incidents which some would call abuse or neglect, but others, just as well meaning, would call more white than black, more indifferent or negligent than criminal (Faulkner, 1982).

Lawrence A. Frolik is Professor of Law at the University of Pittsburgh School of Law, Pittsburgh, PA 15260.

Imagine a spectrum that illustrates the possible behavior of the caregiver of an elderly person. One end represents the very best behavior: love and care. The other end represents the very worst behavior: abuse and neglect. Between these stark opposites rests all the other behavior: some good, some not so good, some bad, some not so bad.

The goal of the law is to move the behavior of the caregivers of the elderly along the spectrum away from abuse or neglect towards the care and love. We criminalize abuse and neglect not to end it, but to reduce its frequency and degree (Van den Haag, 1981). Punishment of those who abuse or neglect the elderly meets our need for retribution. But we also hope that caregivers will learn that they are answerable for their actions and perhaps by criminalizing abuse and neglect we will, over time, minimize it.[1]

But if law is to deter, it must be feared, if not respected. To fear it, or at least its punishments, one must know of it. In short, an unknown law cannot deter. Do elderly caregivers know of the possible criminal consequences of their behavior? Are they aware of the criminal sanctions that can be brought to bear? Indeed, does anyone not linked into the elderly care network know of the existence of the laws against elderly abuse and neglect?[2]

A caregiver must also fear disclosure of abuse before the law can work its deterrence. The unknown criminal cannot be punished. While most other criminals expect that their crime will be known, they hope that their identity will never be revealed. The abuser of the elderly, however, expects that the crime will never be uncovered. All too often the abuser's hope is fulfilled. The abuse is never discovered and the abuser is never brought to justice.

Abuse and neglect laws can be successful only if abusers know they exist, if they fear and expect detection, and if they sufficiently fear the law's retribution. Absent these conditions, laws against abuse and neglect will fail to deter and will operate only retrospectively. While the desire for retribution will be served, the vastly more important value of deterrence will remain unfulfilled. If abuse and neglect laws operate only on past acts and fail to effect future behavior, they must be considered failures. Conversely, if the laws modify the behavior of caregivers, if they move the incidence of behavior away from the criminal and towards the ideal, the laws have been a success.

Our goal is clear. We must increase the probability that abuse and neglect laws are effective by ensuring that caregivers know that such laws exist, by detecting elder abuse and neglect, and by implementing punishments severe enough to cause abusers to modify their behavior.

GUARDIANS AND THE ABUSED ELDERLY

Introduction

Victims of abuse and neglect rarely report it (Katz, 1980). They may be unaware that they are being victimized and have no idea that the law would protect them (U.S. Congress Select Committee on Aging, 1985). A few elderly may believe that the abusive treatment is "normal" or "deserved," or least the best that they can expect.

For many silent victims, a fear to report stems from the possibility of retaliation or from a fear of the loss of the caregiver (even an abusive caregiver may be better than none at all) (Katz, 1980). Other victims, otherwise willing to report the abuse, do not know to whom or how to report the victimization (Katz, 1980). Still others may be so isolated or under the control of the caregiver that they have no opportunity to seek help (Katz, 1980).

For the unknowledgeable, the fearful or the isolated victim, the only hope is detection by outsiders. These victims must rely "on the kindness of strangers." For them, state laws provide for mandatory reporting, investigatory staffs, and for forceable entry.[3]

But there are other victims for whom more is needed, much more. These are the incompetent[4] victims of abuse and neglect. Those who do not understand what is happening to them, who no longer are able to communicate with the larger world. They are the truest victims for they do not even know they are being abused or neglected. But they do know pain, isolation, fear, and emotional oppression. They do have financial assets at risk of theft or misuse. And they do need help.

The Incompetent Victim

Guardianship

The abused or neglected incompetent elderly get help through the guardianship system. Laws against abuse and neglect almost always provide for the appointment of a guardian as a means of assisting (rescuing?) abused victims who cannot help themselves.[5] Of course, guardianship did not originate with the passage of anti-abuse and neglect laws. Guardianship has been a part of the Anglo-American legal tradition for over five hundred years (Frolik, 1981). But only recently has it been incorporated into the scheme of protective services, which is the system by which many anti-abuse and neglect laws operate.[6] Protective services has adopted the traditional guardianship structure as a means of protecting victims of abuse and neglect. The appointment of a guardian allows the removal of the abusive caregiver with the replacement of a "good" caregiver.[7]

Though some guardians are appointed in response to an abusive situation, a far greater number are appointed merely because a need exists for a substituted decision maker and caretaker and not because of abuse or neglect. It is estimated that at any time over 500,000 elderly individuals are under the supervision of a guardian or conservator (Pepper, 1987). In many instances a guardian will act as the caretaker. In other cases, the individual will have a separate guardian and a caretaker. For example, an incompetent individual in a nursing home might have a guardian, but the caretaker will be the nursing home employees. In the context of this paper, however, the guardian is to be thought of as acting as the caretaker of the incompetent ward, or if not the caretaker, then having a close enough personal relationship to the ward to have the opportunity to commit abuse and neglect.

Even if no abuse or neglect have occurred, the appointment of a guardian has, as one of its objectives, the forestalling of future abuse or neglect. For surely no one is more at risk of exploitation than an incompetent individual. Guardianship is the prophylaxis that prevents abuse and neglect. The newer concept of protective services and its older cousin, guardianship, have a certain propinquity. They emanate from the common concern for the well-being of the elderly and share a strong streak of paternalism.

But they diverge sharply in source of authority. Protective services looks to the bureaucratic tradition of executive power that relies upon professionalism. Empowered by the legislature, the executive applies its superior knowledge and resources to protect and promote the commonwealth. The power of the executive is proactive and nondelegatory. The employee (actor) for a protective service agency does not act on behalf of the elderly abused or neglected client, nor is the employee necessarily responsive to the client. Bureaucratic actors answer only to those in their chain-of-command, to their superiors who in turn answer to the chief executive, the governor. Although a protective service agency may choose to listen to clients and to follow their suggestions, the agency does so only voluntarily and only because it has elected such a policy. Even if the protective service agency considers itself to be responsive to those that it serves, in truth the agency is answerable to the executive. The agency is the creature of the executive and has such freedom only as the executive allows. Indeed, client autonomy is a fiction. It exists only at the sufferance of the protective services agency.

Guardianship finds its authority in the powers of the courts who have been granted the authority by the legislature to appoint guardians for the incompetent.[8] Under it parens patriae power, the state has authorized courts to appoint guardians to make decisions for the mentally incompetent (Frolik, 1981). The power of the guardian is a delegation of the power of the court. The right of the guardian to act can be no greater than the right of the judge who appointed the guardian. Indeed, depending upon how much authority the court has granted the guardian, the scope of the guardian's power may be a good deal less than that of the appointing judge.[9] But whatever the extent of the guardian's authority, the guardian remains answerable to the appointing court. Most importantly, the guardian is answerable only to the court. Though the guardian acts on behalf of the incompetent ward, the guardian is not answerable to the ward, but to the appointing court.[10]

The Incompetent, the Guardian, and the Court

The court that appointed the guardian is responsible for the acts of the guardian and only the court has the authority to supervise the performance of the guardian. While others may complain or inform the court of the shortcomings of the guardian, only the court may act to compel the guardian to modify his or her behavior. If the guardian mistreats the ward,[11] the guardian is at fault. But ultimately, a failure of the guardian is a failure of the court. Guardians can commit a single wrong act or they can repeatedly misperform. It is the not the former that concerns us or for which we would hold the court responsible. Imagine a 40 year old woman who is the guardian for her 77 year old aunt who suffers from early stage Alzheimer's disease. The aunt lives with her guardian. One day the aunt is particularly difficult to deal with. The guardian in a fit of anger locks her ill-tempered ward in her room for the day to punish her. By the end of the day the guardian, now contrite, releases her aunt and never again treats her that way. (The guardian hires a practical nurse to assist in the care of her aunt.) While this might be an incident of abuse, and while the court as supervisor of the guardian is technically responsible, one is not inclined to "blame" the court on account of an isolated act of abuse by the guardian.

No, what we are after here is the repeat performer, the guardian whose pattern of performance consistently falls below the acceptable standard. The guardian who routinely misappropriates the assets of the ward, who repeatedly neglects or abuses the ward, or the guardian who has never heard of Alzheimer's and treats the stricken ward as if he or she were a willful, disobedient child. It is these chronic malperforming guardians for whom we hold the appointing court responsible. Its the abuse and neglect of their wards for whom we lay the ultimate responsibility at the feet of the court.

THE ABUSIVE GUARDIAN

The chronic misperformance by a guardian may indicate that the court either selected an inappropriate guardian, failed to train the guardian properly or failed to supervise the guardian effectively. In a word, the court is responsible for the selection, training and supervision of guardians. Alternatively, the court may have performed admirably in all these functions, but the guardian nevertheless misperformed and successfully masked the malfeasance from the court. Even if that were the case, we would question the quality of the court's supervision since in most instances the court should discover a misperforming guardian.

Do courts fail in these appointive and supervisory tasks? Given the lack of human perfection, it seems safe to assume that they do. But how frequently this occurs is difficult to answer. The true test of the selection, training and supervision of courts is in the behavior of the guardian. If the guardians perform well, it hardly seems relevant that the courts may have selected badly, trained poorly or supervised inadequately. But if the guardians' performance is subpar, we ought to take a careful look at the performance of the appointing court.

Grading a Guardian

To determine how well guardians perform is not an easy task. Suppose that we were given the task to evaluate the performance of noninstitutional guardians.[12] Consider the obstacles. We would first have to agree as to what constitutes "subpar" performance by a guardian. It is doubtful that any objective standard could be developed. It is possible that useful standards of measurement of guardianship of property could be developed. For example, we might ask, were the ward's assets collected and protected? Were the assets productively invested? Were the assets properly expended? Was the ward maintained manner consistent with the value of the assets? Did the guardian keep adequate records?

But a moment's reflection reveals how subjective are these apparently "hard data" questions. What does it mean to adequately protect assets if the assets are personal or real property? Imagine a 72 year old ward, Wendy, who is a widow with two children, Sam age 50, and Dot age 54. Sam has been appointed guardian of Wendy's estate. Suppose Wendy owns a weekend home in the mountains 90 miles from her residence. Now incompetent from what appears to be Alzheimer's disease, she can no longer make use of her weekend home. Her two adult children, however, have been frequent users of the home prior to their mother's illness. Sam, as guardian, continues to maintain the weekend home and both he and his sister, Dot, continue to use it on weekends. Is Sam abusing his position? He might claim that Wendy might recover and so he must maintain the weekend home. He might argue that he is only maintaining the status quo that existed before his mother's illness. Finally, he might protest that because he and Dot are the likely heirs, no one is harmed by the maintenance and use of the weekend home. Should Sam be considered to be acting in a subpar fashion? Is he guilty of "abuse?"[13]

Consider other hypotheticals. Suppose that prior to the onset of incompetency, a ward always made lavish Christmas gifts to her grandchildren. Her guardian-daughter proposes to continue the tradition even though to do so means that the guardian would make gifts of the ward's assets to the guardian's children. If questioned about the propriety of such actions, the guardian might reply that the ward, her mother, would have wanted it that way. What if the ward prior to her incapacity had kept ten dogs as pets. Should the guardian continue to maintain the dogs even for a comatose ward? Some might think it wasteful while others might think it an appropriate adherence to the wishes of the ward.

When we move from financial guardianship issues to personal care issues the waters become even murkier. Just what constitutes appropriate care for an incompetent individual is often at issue. Take, for example, the perennial issue of whether to leave an incompetent ward in his or her own home or to move him or her to a congregate care facility or to a nursing home. While our emotions urge us to leave the ward at home, financial realities and health care concerns may call for supportive living arrangements. Who is to judge the decision of the guardian in such cases? Even the guardian may be unsure whether the proper decision was made.

Too many of the decisions that a guardian must make are not susceptible to easy critique. They are not black and white issues, but swirling shades of gray. The "correct" outcome is impossible to identify among the interacting and competing cultural, social and personal values, the emotional limitations and compulsions that act upon the guardian, and the financial limitations and realities that further constrict the choices of the guardian. Given such complexity, to blandly label a guardian's behavior as "sub-par" is simplistic and misleading. At best, we might identify particular acts of the guardian as "unwise" or "of dubious merit."

Even if we felt certain acts of the guardian were wrong (though not illegal nor constituting elder abuse), we would also have to admit that many other acts of the guardian were "correct." Faced with a guardian whose actions are of a decidedly mixed quality, some good, some not so good, it is very unclear how we should grade the guardian. For guardians, just like other caregivers, cannot be pinned to a particular performance point (for example, a grade of 85 on a scale of 100). Rather, guardians, as with all actors, operate over a range of behavior. Certainly some guardians operate over a range that is closer to the ideal than do others. But every guardian will have the off day and will act in a manner that, in retrospective, was most unwise (perhaps even in the eyes of the guardian). And if it is difficult to "grade" any individual decision, it is much more perplexing to give a single grade to a range of behavior.

Abusive Guardians

Let us abandon, then, the apparently intractable goal of grading guardians. Instead, let us focus our attention upon a narrower, yet more critical, issue of whether guardians are guilty of abuse and neglect of their wards. Here we have a standard to guide us: the state law against abuse and neglect. Within the law we will find prohibitions against "injury," "confinement," "sexual harassment," or punishment that results in "physical harm or mental anguish." Acts such as these are surely identifiable. To be sure, the prohibitions are not always self-defining. At the margins, we may find it difficult to say confidently that a particular act constitutes abuse. But as state statutes are interpreted and applied over time, we should gain a more precise understanding of just what behavior constitutes abuse and neglect. Of course, it is irrelevant for our purposes whether the exact point at which abuse begins remains indeterminate. For we are not interested in the precise assessment of performance. We should be just as concerned with a guardian whose behavior is near the point of abuse as with a guardian who crosses the line and is an actual abuser.

Suppose we wanted to survey guardians to discover what percent (if any) act in an abusive manner. To do so would be difficult. We cannot just ask guardians if they are guilty of abuse and neglect. Who would be so foolish as to admit it? Instead, we might ask guardians to describe how they behave. Possibly a few of the abusers would believe that their behavior was acceptable and so might reveal illegal acts. But most would probably conceal abusive behavior.

We might ask to observe the guardians in action, but this would be very time consuming, very expensive and not necessarily reliable. A guardian, as with anyone under observation, will improve his or her behavior and will surely try to eliminate abusive behavior. Again, a few guardians would not realize that their behavior is unacceptable or illegal, but they would be a distinct minority. We might also approach the wards and ask them how they are being treated by the guardian. Some might be able to give a coherent answer, but most, because of their incapacity, would be highly unreliable commentators.

Empirical evidence of abusive guardians, therefore, will be hard to come by. The absence of direct evidence of guardian abuse does not mean we lack any evidence that guardians might abuse. We know that of those that commit elder abuse or neglect, the largest number are related to the victim. Similarly, the overwhelming majority of abusers are the victim's caregiver (Katz, 1980). We need only match those statistics with the knowledge that many, if not a majority, of noninstitutional guardians are related to their wards and many guardians act as caregivers. If some related caregivers commit abuse, it would seem probable that some related caregiver guardians also commit abuse.

Guardians who are related to their ward may be less prone to commit abuse than other caregivers because guardians are more likely to have voluntarily assumed their responsibilities. While some unpaid caregivers will have consciously volunteered for the job, others will have the duties thrust upon them as a result of an emergency. Still others will find themselves in the role as they gradually take on more and more responsibility for the dependent individual. Conversely, courts appoint guardians, and no one will be appointed a guardian without their consent. Many guardians will be "true" volunteers. By that, we mean that they willingly stepped forward to assume the role of guardian. Others are more reluctant. They serve because no one else would do so. They may not wish to serve as guardian, but because of their sense of obligation to the incompetent elderly individual they reluctantly accept the responsibility.

While abusive guardians might come from either the ranks of the genuinely willing or the reluctant guardian, it seems more likely that abusive guardians would be more prevalent in the ranks of the nonvoluntary guardian. For it is these guardians who are more likely to resent the burden of the ward and feel that they have been imposed upon. They might resent the appointing court or they might resent other relatives of the ward who were spared the burden of acting as the guardian. They might believe that by being the guardian they have taken on a disproportionate burden. Not being able to take out their resentment against the court or the other relatives, they may take it out against the ward.

Not all nonvoluntary guardians take on their role with a disgruntled attitude. Indeed, some may begin the duty with a willing disposition to do the right thing, but they may not be temperamentally suited to be a guardian. Perhaps the appointing court was aware of the potential unsuitability of the individual to act as guardian, but in the absence of any other guardian, the court had no choice but to appoint the individual. At first, the guardian may perform appropriately. But over time, the strain of being a guardian may begin to unravel the good intentions of the guardian. Later, the worst fears of the court may be realized, when the guardian begins to abuse the ward.

Some guardians, whether voluntary or not, may abuse or neglect their ward and yet may not do so deliberately. These are guardians who are unknowledgeable about how to care for an incompetent elderly ward. They may sincerely believe that a low level of custodial care is sufficient and unknowningly allow the ward to be cared for in a manner that approaches abuse. A few may believe that it is a waste of resources to provide decent care for an elderly incompetent ward and may believe that their actions reflect the accepted societal view. Some guardians will be more negligent than culpable and commit abuse or its near equivalent out of inertia, laziness or due to the press of other responsibilities. A few noncaretaker guardians may inadvertently commit abuse by their failure to adequately supervise the actions of the caretaker of the ward.

Other guardians may be conscious that they are remiss in the manner that they treat their ward, but believe that the incompetent ward deserves no better. We could almost say that as a cultural matter such guardians do not perceive their actions as being wrong. If questioned about the level of care that they provided, these guardians might respond defensively that they were doing nothing wrong. They lack the moral sensitivity to realize that an elderly incompetent deserves more humane treatment.

A few guardians who begin well enough, may become morally desensitized over time. At the beginning of their guardianship, they may have tried to treat the ward in an acceptable manner. But gradually they permit their standards to slip as the reality of the burden of guardianship became more apparent or more burdensome (Steinmetz, 1980). The duties of guardianship, in effect, degrade them and dulls their moral sensitivity. What they would have condemned at the beginning of the guardianship, by degrees becomes bearable and, at last, the norm. The deterioration of their standards is justified by the adoption of the attitude that they give the ward all that he or she deserves.

Other guardians, like many abusers, may react to the difficulty of the personality of the ward and respond in kind. While the ward may not be abusive, the ward may act in a manner that is rude, provoking or exasperating. The guardian, not trained in how to handle an incompetent ward, loses patience and loses self-control and begins to "retaliate" against the ward. The guardian justifies the abuse in the belief that the ward "deserves" it or "asked for it" (U.S. Congress Select Committee on Aging, 1985).

Like any abuser of the elderly, guardians can be prosecuted under state abuse and neglect statutes. Their guardian status gives them no special protection or defense from criminal or civil liability. But does a guardian have a heightened degree of responsibility? By virtue of the fact that they are a guardian, can we hold them to a higher standard of care? Examination of the state abuse and neglect statutes yields a negative answer. Nothing in the statutes suggests or requires that guardians are held to a higher standard than other care-givers.[14]

Judicial Response

Right to Penalize Guardians Who Misperform

Although not held to a higher standard of behavior under state's abuse and neglect statutes, guardians are accountable to a second authority: the appointing court. Unlike the abuse and neglect laws which provide penalties for the abuser, however, the court that appoints a guardian may lack the power to penalize the abuser. State guardianship statutes are the source of the court's power to appoint guardian. While these statutes permit the court to remove the guardian for malfeasance, they generally do not provide for the court to fine or otherwise penalize the guardian. A court, faced with guardian malfeasance, has few options short of outright removal. If the guardian has embezzled, misappropriated or mishandled the assets of the ward, the court can order restitution. But if the guardian has physically or psychologically abused or neglected the ward, the court can only remove the guardian. The ward, acting through a successor guardian or a guardian ad litem, can sue the former guardian for civil damages. The appointing court, however, has no independent cause of action against the guardian.

The lack of a judicial cause of action against a misperforming guardian probably has little direct effect on the behavior of guardians. The combined deterrent effect of possible civil liability to the ward and the criminal and civil liabilities possible under state abuse and neglect statutes should be sufficient to give pause to any guardian suspectible to deterrence. Of course, this assumes that the guardian realizes the potential civil and criminal liability from maltreating a ward. A guardian who is ignorant of the consequences cannot be deterred. The addition of liability to the appointing court would mean nothing to a guardian unaware of it.

Liability to the appointing court could be effective, however, if the guardian is made specifically aware of it. Imagine, for example, a guardian who is only vaguely aware, if at all of his or her civil or criminal liability for abuse of the ward. The creation of possible judicial sanctions by the appointing court could ensure that guardians are aware of the societal approbation of mistreatment of wards. Suppose that the state guardianship statute specifically provided that the appointing court can fine a guardian who mistreats a ward.[15] It would only remain for the court to instruct the guardian about the possibility of judicial punishment should the guardian misbehave. Now we would have the situation of a guardian who is aware of the cost of mistreatment of the ward. Even if the guardian remained ignorant of the other possible liabilities, he or she would at least know that the appointing court could impose a penalty for mistreatment of the ward.

Moreover, the guardian might well wonder and ask just what is considered "mistreatment of a ward." As the guardian listens to the court describe the penalties that it can inflict upon the guardian who misbehaves, we might expect the guardian to ask the court to clarify just what sort of acts might lead to punishment by the court. Presumedly, any judge who takes the time to instruct the guardian as to possible penalties would also take the time to tell the guardian what kind of behavior is expected.

Training and Education of the Guardian

Before courts can begin to fine errant guardians, they must first decide what is inappropriate behavior. They might define it as behavior that would violate the state protection from abuse and neglect laws. Yet that would be redundant and give the wrong message to the guardian. For we want the guardian to do more than merely avoid criminal behavior. We want the guardian to strive towards the ideal, to clearly avoid treatment of the ward that in any way approaches abuse and neglect. What the court needs are standards that encourage the guardian behavior away from the bad (abuse and neglect) and towards the good. The ultimate goal is to move the bell curve of guardian behavior towards the ideal end of the continuum.

The court should not be satisfied merely to diminish or even eliminate unlawful behavior by a few guardians. Those guardians whose behavior is in the "gray" range (not so good, not so bad) should also be encouraged to improve their performance. The court needs to instruct guardians as to how they should perform in the hope that all will behave a little (or even a lot) better. It is not sufficient to exhort the guardian to "do well." The court must instruct the guardian as to what is appropriate behavior. Provide a "role model," if you will. Once the court has instructed the guardian on how to perform, it is then appropriate to inform the guardian as to the possible consequences of the failure to perform, i.e., fines.

Instruction of the guardian should not be thought of merely as a lecture from the bench. Rather, the court ought to have a prepared set of materials and qualified personnel who can acquaint the guardian with his or her responsibilities. No guardian should be "turned loose," with little or no judicial guidance, as far too many are at present. While a guardian should not need a formal course of instruction as to how to perform, a guardian could profit from an hour or two of instruction and advice. The court could supply the guardian with printed material and perhaps show a videotape that explains what is expected of a guardian (with a concise, but clear, statement of possible penalties for misbehavior). The guardian should also have access to informational support during the term of the guardianship. Not necessarily a "guardian hotline," but someone in the court system to call when advice is needed. In short, if we want guardians to perform better, we must give them support and not just appoint and forget them.

Why courts have not taken a stronger role in the education of guardians is a bit of a mystery. Lack of support staff and the cost of doing so are undoubtedly major factors. Yet the courts for the most part have not been aggressive in seeking the funding necessary to do the job. We simply do not hear from judges that they lack the resources to properly prepare guardians for their duties. The judicial silence may be grounded in the belief that the petitioner's attorney will point the guardian out on the right path. Although no studies exist to so prove, it seems likely that the great majority of guardians (individual, that is) are also the petitioners who seek the judicial finding of incompetency. For example, the daughter of the incompetent father files the petition with the court with the request that the father be declared incompetent and that she, the daughter be declared his guardian.

It is also most certainly true that almost all petitioners are represented by counsel. While in theory no lawyer may be needed to file a petition for guardianship, in practice almost every petition will be presented by one. The judge, seeing that an attorney is handling things, may unconsciously (or even consciously) assume that the lawyer will answer the guardian's questions as to what to do, when to do it, and to whom it should be done. That assumption may be true as long as the lawyer is involved with the case. In the beginning, the lawyer may well guide the fledgling guardian. But the lawyer is not likely to remain in the case. Once the petition for guardianship is successful, the lawyer will be paid for his or her efforts and be seen no more. Oh, the lawyer may accept an occasional call for help from the guardian, but if the calls become too frequent, the lawyer will charge for the answer. Few guardians will be willing to pay the lawyer at the prevailing hourly fee. Instead, the guardian will foresake professional advice and sail alone across the uncharted guardianship waters.

It falls, then, to the courts to accept the responsibility to properly train guardians.[16] If the courts lack the resources to do so, they must tell the legislature of their financial need. While a plea for money to train guardians may not stir the legislature, an argument that the training of guardians may reduce abuse and neglect and lead to better treatment of wards may be better received. The courts must also request the right to fine guardians who mistreat their wards or neglect their duties. The combination of training and the threat of punishment should go far to improving the performance of guardians. But it is not nearly enough.

Supervision and Review

Even if the courts receive adequate funding and authority to train and discipline guardians, more needs to be done. The best safeguard against guardian abuse and neglect and the best way to insure that guardians perform in an adequate manner is for the court to review periodically the performance of the guardian. The court must have the authority and resources to supervise the guardians that it appoints. Today, the exact opposite is almost always the case. The courts lack the resources and the authority to adequately supervise the guardians that they appoint. In a way, it is almost unbelieveable that the court can appoint a guardian with wide powers over the life of the ward and yet have no way to insure that the guardian behaves properly.

Such supervision that the courts provide occurs almost exclusively at the termination of the guardian's reign, be that at the death of the ward, the death of the guardian or the resignation of the guardian. Traditionally, courts have expected the guardian to sum up and account for what had occurred during the period of the guardianship. For guardians of the estate, the court can demand a complete and detailed accounting of all income and expenditures. Of course, if the guardian misperformed, the after the fact accounting would only reveal the past transgressions. It would do nothing to monitor the on-going performance of the guardian. To be sure, the guardian might be financially liable for any misperformance, but to collect damages from the guardian might be very difficult.

As for guardians of the person, supervision, even after the fact, is often very minimal. In most states, guardians of the person have no duty to report on a regular basis to the court. A few states require periodic reports, but most are content to assume that all is well.[17] Presumedly if anything goes wrong, the court will hear of it. Otherwise, the guardian carries on his or her duties without judicial interference or supervision. At the end of the guardianship, the guardian has to account to the court. Unlike a guardian of the estate, however, a guardian of the person will generally not be required to give the court a detailed description of how he or she treated the ward. If the guardianship ends because of the death of the ward, it is doubtful whether the court expects any meaningful description of the performance of the guardian. The death of the ward (unless under circumstances that might call the guardian's behavior into question) in effect moots the issue as to how the guardian performed.

If the guardianship ends because the guardian wishes to resign, the court might be more curious about how he or she performed. If, for example, the guardian requests to resign because of a conflict of personalities with the ward, the court might inquire as to the quality of care provided by the guardian. But most state guardianship statutes do not require any special report from a guardian who wishes to resign. In fact, most state guardianship statutes are silent as to the kind of information that a guardian must supply either during or upon the termination of a guardianship.[18]

What is missing in most states is the concept of periodic reports by the guardian to the court. Absent such reports, the court cannot properly supervise the guardian. As a result, the guardian is essentially a free actor, effectively answerable to no one. While some guardians will perform at their best without supervision, others will perform less effectively than they would if they knew that they would have to answer for their actions. Can we prove this assertion? Probably not, but it seems human nature to relax if no one is watching. It does not mean that an unsupervised guardian will abuse or neglect the ward. It is simply the commonsense assertion that guardians would perform better if they were supervised.

Need for Additional Resources

Courts can monitor guardians in a variety of ways, but less important than what they do is that they have the will to do it. If the courts are serious about the quality of care provided by guardians, the courts must pressure the legislature to give them the authority and the resources necessary to supervise guardians. For example, if the courts want annual reports from the guardian, they must also have the personnel to review those reports, otherwise, the reports will merely gather dust on some clerk's desk.

An annual report from the guardian could be very useful if it is reviewed by someone with the necessary training and sufficient time. If an annual guardian report is merely going to be placed in a file, unread or at most given a cursory review, it is nothing but a palliative that squanders the guardian's time and energy. The judge cannot be expected to provide meaningful oversight of the reports. As a practical matter judges lack the time to review yet another piece of paper. They must be provided with adequate support personnel to review reports filed by the guardian.

Since the judges lack the time to review the guardian's report, it is the judges who should be demanding additional assistance. It is the judges who should impress upon the legislature the danger to the elderly wards of allowing guardians to go unsupervised. In essence, the judges must say to the legislature, "You cannot hold us responsible for the quality of care provided by the guardians that we appoint unless you give us the necessary resources to monitor the performance of the guardians."

Court Visitors

If, by some unforeseen event, the legislature does grant the courts sufficient support to supervise guardians, what should be done? While reports from the guardian would be a start, they would not necessarily uncover abuse and neglect or even substandard performance by the guardian. Clever guardians would surely dissemble and not reveal any wrong doing. Even guardians who did not believe that they have done anything wrong are likely to put a gloss upon the past year's actions when reporting to the court. The only sure way to know how guardians performs is to observe them in action.

Use of a Court Visitor

Courts that appoint guardians need the authority and, more importantly, the financial resources to employ court visitors who review the behavior of guardians. The visitor would perform as the eyes of the court to monitor the guardians. Unlike the passivity of guardian submitted reports, the visitor would be out "in the field" inspecting the actions of the guardian. The visitor would inspect the ward's living arrangements, inspect the ward's financial records, talk to the ward (if possible), and prepare a report to the court. Armed with the visitor's report, the court could take appropriate action against a malperforming guardian.

If the court has a visitor's report, the relationship between the guardian and the court changes rather dramatically. To the guardian, the court would no longer be a distant and ineffectual overseer, but would be an effective supervisor and a protector of the rights of the ward. Guardians who have any control over their behavior (some may be pathologically incapable of not abusing the ward) would surely modify it to reduce or eliminate abuse if there was any chance of discovery of the abuse by the court appointed visitor. All guardians, whether abusers or not, might well reconsider how they treat the ward if they know that they may have to account for their actions. The use of visitors, then, would not only uncover abuse, but their use would result in a general improvement in the quality of guardianship.

A system of court appointed visitors could be quite expensive. A number of visitors would be required. A careful review of the treatment of a ward could be quite time consuming so that each visitor could handle only a limited number of cases.[19] An additional expense would arise from the need to train and supervise the visitors. The cost of a visitor program might well make it prohibitive.

Two ways suggest themselves to reduce the cost to the state. First, the estate of the incompetent ward could be charged for the cost of the visitor. The amount charged could be on a sliding scale in proportion to the the size of the incompetent's estate.[20] In this manner, the ward, who is the beneficiary of the visitor, would help bear the costs of the program. If the state is unwilling to bear any of the costs of a visitor program, individual wards, who could afford to pay, could be charged an amount in excess of the actual cost as a means of offsetting the costs of indigent wards too poor to pay for a visitor.

Whether it is wise to force wards as a group to absorb the cost of a visitor system is a matter of public policy. A reasonable case can be made to require those wards who can afford to do so should reimburse the state for the cost of a visitor. It seems fair to charge a price for a benefit received. But is more problematical whether affluent wards should bear the costs of visitors for the poorer wards. If we as a society decide that wards will have visitors, regardless of whether they can afford them, it would seem only right that society, and not the more affluent wards, pay the cost of visitors for indigent wards.

The cost of the visitorship, whether paid for by the wards, by the society, or both, could be greatly reduced if visitors visited wards on a selected basis. Instead of the visitor periodically visiting every ward, visitors could investigate only those wards designated by the court. The time and energy of the visitors could be focused on those wards thought by the court to be at risk. Prime candidates to be visited, for example, would include wards with guardians who were reluctant to accept the position, wards living with guardians, and wards with significant assets. If the court required periodic reports from the guardian, such reports would also be excellent indicators as to which wards might be useful to visit. Over time the visitors could be expected to develop a profile of the characteristics of wards for whom a visit is most valuable. In short, the system would learn to identify the wards who are at risk.

In addition to visits of selected wards, the visitors should also visit a number of randomly selected wards. This would allow the courts to warn all guardians that they might be subjected to an inspection by a court appointed visitor. Such a warning ought to at least marginally improve the behavior of the guardians. Random selection also would serve as a source of information about what characteristics of wards warrant a visitation. It would also offer some protection for mistreated or abused wards who did not fit the profile of being at risk.

Armed with the report of the visitor, the court would be in a position to take appropriate action against guardians who failed to perform their duties with the proper diligence, vigor and concern. The court response could vary from a mere admonition of the guardian, to removal, or even a fine (assuming that the court is given the authority to penalize guardians).

CONCLUSION

The combination of the training of guardianships, proper court supervision of guardians, and the right of the court to discipline guardians would constitute a change in the current relationship in most jurisdictions between courts and guardians. No more would the court merely appoint the guardian and thereafter have no role to play. No longer would the guardian be essentially a free actor, almost accountable to no one. With visitorship and potential penalties, guardians would truely become the agents of the court. Unless we assume that courts would be indifferent to the wards' quality of life, such a system should mean better treatment of elderly, incompetent wards. And although we would still live in a world of grays, we would have moved a little closer to the light and a little farther from the dark.

ENDNOTES

1. The following states have criminalized the abuse and neglect of older persons. Ala. Code § 38-9-7 (Supp. 1988); Ark. Stat. Ann. § 5-28-103 (1987); Fla. Stat. Ann. § 415.111 (Supp. 1989); Ga. Code Ann. § 30-5-8 (1986); Minn. Stat. § 626.557 (1988); Nev. Rev. Stat. Ann. § 200.5099 (Michie 1986 § Supp. 1988); R.I. Gen. Laws § 23-17.8-10 (Supp. 1988); S.C. Code Ann. § 43-29-41 & -100 (1976); S.D. Codified Laws Ann. § 22-46-2 to 3 (1988 & Supp. 1989); Tenn. Code Ann. S 71-6-117 (1987 & Supp. 1988); Utah Code Ann. § 62A-3-302 (Supp. 1988); Vt. Stat. Ann. tit. 18 § 1159 (Supp. 1988); W. Va. Code § 9-6-15 (Supp. 1988); Wisc. Stat. Ann. § 940.285-.29 (West Supp. 1988); Wyo. Stat. § 35-20-109 (1988). States which do not specifically *criminalize* abuse and neglect but have provision regarding reporting abuse to prosecutor or police for criminal investigation. Conn. Gen. Stat. Ann. § 46a-24 (1986 & Supp. 1988); Haw. Rev. Stat. § 349C-3 (1985 & Supp. 1988); Idaho Code § 39-5310 (1985); Ky. Rev. Stat. Ann. § 209.150 (Michie/Bobbs-Merrill 1985); La. Rev. Stat. Ann. § 14:403.2 (West 1986); N.H. Rev. Stat. Ann. § 161-D:4 (Supp. 1988); N.J. Stat. Ann. § 52:27G-7.2 (West 1986 & Supp. 1988).

2. If the lack of scholarly attention to the problem in law reviews is any indication, the criminalization of abuse and neglect has received relatively little publicity at least in the legal community. In the last five years (1983 through 1988) only seven articles have been published on the topic of "Elder Abuse" in law reviews.

3. Between 1980 and 1985, twenty-four states either amended existing statutes or enacted some form of mandatory reporting legislation. (Note, Fordham Urban L.J., 1986)

4. An incompetent individual is one who from a legal standpoint the state may take actions that limit the "individual's right to make decisions about his person or property based on his mental disability." (Brakel, Parry, & Weiner, 1985) The definition of legal incompetency differs from state to state, but in general state statutes define legal incompetency as an inability to make or communicate responsible decisions.

5. Guardianship is also used to force "help" upon a reluctant elderly person who would rather be left alone. These are the so-called victims of self-neglect or abuse. The issues raised by helping those who do not want help are beyond the purview of this article.

6. The following states have adopted protective services legislation. Ala. Code §§ 38-9-1 to-11 (Supp. 1988); Alaska Stat. §§ 47.24.010-.100 (1984); Ariz. Rev. Stat. Ann. §§ 46-451 to-454 (1988); Ark. Stat. Ann. §§ 5-28-101 to-215 (1987); Cal. Welf. & Inst. Code §§ 15600-15650 (Deering Supp. 1989); Colo. Rev. Stat. §§ 26-3.1-101 to-105 (Supp. 1988); Conn. Gen. Stat. Ann. §§ 46a-14 to -25 (1986 & Supp. 1988); Del. Code Ann. tit. 31, §§ 3901-3911 (1985 & Supp. 1988); D.C. Code Ann. §§ 6-2501 to -2513 (Supp. 1988); Fla. Stat. Ann. § 415.101-.113 (West 1987 & Supp. 1989); Ga. Code Ann. § 30-5-1 to -8 (1986); Haw. Rev. Stat. §§ 349C-1 to -8 (1985 & Supp. 1988); Idaho Code §§ 29-5301 to

-5312 (1985); Ill. Ann. Stat. ch. 23, para. 6501-6510 (Smith-Hurd 1988); Ind. Code Ann. § 4-28-5-1 to -13 (Burns Supp. 1988); Iowa Code § 235B.1-.2 (1985 & Supp. 1988); Kan. Stat. Ann. § 39-1421 to 1429 (1986); Ky. Rev. Stat. Ann. §§ 209.010-.160 (Michie/Bobbs-Merrill 1985); La. Rev. Stat. Ann. § 14:403.2 (West 1986); Me. Rev. Stat. Ann. tit. 22 §§ 3470-3487 (West Supp. 1988); Md. Fam. Law Code Ann. §§ 14-101 to -404 (1984 & Supp. 1988); Mass. Gen. Laws Ann. ch. 19A §§ 14-26 (West Supp. 1989); Mich. Comp. Laws Ann. §§ 400.11a-.11f (West 1988); Minn. Stat. § 626.557 (1988); Miss. Code Ann. §§ 43-47-1 to -35 (Supp. 1988); Mo. Ann. Stat. §§ 660.250-.295 (Vernon 1988); Mont. Code Ann. §§ 53-5-202 to -205 (1988); Neb. Rev. Stat. §§ 28-348 to -387 (Supp. 1988); Nev. Rev. Stat. Ann. §§ 200.5091-.5099 (Michie 1986 & Supp. 1988); N.H. Rev. Stat. Ann. §§ 161-D:1-8 (Supp. 1988); N.J. Stat. Ann. §§ 52:27G-1 to -16 (West 1986 & Supp. 1988); N.M. Stat. Ann. §§ 27-7-1 to -13 (1984); N.Y. Soc. Serv. Law §§ 473-473c (McKinney 1983 & Supp. 1989); N.C. Gen. Stat. §§ 108A-99 to -111 (1988); N.D. Cent. Code §§ 14-07.1-01 to -09 (1981 & Supp. 1987); Ohio Rev. Code §§ 5101.60-.71 (1989); Okla. Stat. tit. 43a § 10-101 to -110 (Supp. 1989); Or. Rev. Stat. §§ 410.610-.990 (1987); 35 Pa. Cons. Stat. Ann. §§ 10211-10223 (Purdon Supp. 1988); R.I. Gen. Laws § 23-27.8-1 to -10 (Supp. 1988) *clause in health facilities; S.C. Code Ann. §§ 43-29-10 to -100 (1976); S.D. Codified Laws Ann. §§ 22-46-1 to -4 (1988 & Supp. 1989) *no section of reporting clause; Tenn. Code Ann. §§ 71-6-101 to -118 (1987 & Supp. 1988); Tex. Hum. Res. Code Ann. §§ 48.001-.84 (Vernon Supp. 1989); Utah Code Ann. §§ 62A-3-301 to -312 (Supp. 1988); Vt. Stat. Ann. tit. 18 §§ 1150-1155 (1982 & Supp. 1988); Va. Code Ann. §§ 63.1-55.3 to .6 (1987 & Supp. 1988); Wash. Rev. Code Ann. §§ 74.34.010-.901 (Supp. 1989); W. Va. Code §§ 9-6-1 to -15 (Supp. 1988); Wisc. Stat. Ann. §§ 940.285-.29 (West Supp. 1988) after 7/1/89 948.20; Wyo. Stat. §§ 35-20-101 to 109 (1988).

7. In many instances, when no private guardian is available a public guardian will be employed or paid by the state to act as the guardian. If the incompetent has sufficient assets, the state may surcharge the incompetent's estate for the cost of the guardian. As of 1988, 19 states had adopted some form of public guardianship. Not all states that provide for protective services provide for public guardians.

8. The following is a list of state statutes that provide for guardianship. Ala. Code §§ 26-2-1 to 26-6-6 (Supp. 1988); Alaska Stat. §§ 13:26:010-.155 (1984); Ariz. Rev. Stat. Ann. §§ 14-5301 to 5314 (1978 & Supp. 1987); Ark. Stat. Ann. §§ 28-65-101 to 603, 28-67-101 to 111 (1987 & Supp. 88); Cal. Prob. Code §§ 1500-1601, 1800-1910, 2100-2808 (Deering 1981 & Supp. 1989); Colo. Rev. Stat. §§ 15-14-301 to 314 (1974 & Supp. 1988); Conn. Gen. Stat. Ann. §§ 45-70 to 77(b) (1981 & Supp. 1988); Del. Code Ann. tit. 12 §§ 3901-3947 (1985); D.C. Code Ann. §§ 21-1501 to 1507 (1981 & Supp. 1988); Fla. Stat. Ann. §§ 744.101-.652 (West 1986 & Supp. 1989); Ga. Code Ann. §§ 29-8-1 to -7 (1986 & Supp. 1989); Haw. Rev. Stat. §§ 56015-101 to 501 (1985 & Supp. 1988); Idaho Code §§ 15-5-301-432 (1985 & Supp. 1988); Ill. Ann. Stat. ch. 110 1/2 13-1 to -5 (Smith-Hurd 1988 & Supp. 1989); Ind. Code Ann. §§ 29-3-1-1 to 29-3-13-3

(Burns Supp. 1989); Iowa Code §§ 633.552-.682 (1985 & Supp. 1989); Kan. Stat. Ann. § 59-3001 to 3038 (1986 & Supp. 1988); Ky. Rev. Stat. Ann. §§ 387.010-.990 (Michie/Bobbs-Merrill 1985); La. Rev. Stat. Ann. §§ 389-426 (West 1986 & Supp. 1989); Me. Rev. Stat. Ann. tit. 18A §§ 5-301 to -313 (West 1986 & Supp. 1988); Md. Est. & Trusts Code Ann. 13-201 to 222, 13-801 to -806 (1984 & Supp. 1988); Mass. Gen. Laws Ann. ch. 201 §§ 6-49 (1987 & Supp. 1989); Mich. Comp. Laws Ann. §§ 330.1600-1642, 700.441-499 (West 1988 & Supp. 1989); Minn. Stat. § 525.54-.614 (1988 & Supp. 1989); Miss. Code Ann. § 93-13-121 to -267 (1972 & Supp. 1989); Mo. Ann. Stat. §§ 475.010-.340 (Vernon 1988 & Supp. 1989); Mont. Code Ann. §§ 72-5-301 to -439 (1988); Neb. Rev. Stat. §§ 30-2617 to -2672 (1943); Nev. Rev. Stat. Ann. 159.013-.215 (Michie 1986 & Supp. 1988); N.H. Rev. Stat. Ann. §§ 464-A:l to 44 (1983 & Supp. 1988); N.J. Stat. Ann. §§ 3B:12-24 to 66 (West 1986 & Supp. 1989); N.M. Stat. Ann. §§ 45-5-301 to 432 (1984 & Supp. 1988); N.Y. Mental Hyg. Law §§ 77.01-.41, 78.01-.31 (McKinney 1983); N.C. Gen. Stat. §§ 35A-1120 to -1361 (1988); N.D. Cent. Code §§ 30.1-26-01 to 30.1-29-32 (1976 & Supp. 1987); Ohio Rev. Stat. §§ 2111:01-471 (1976 & Supp. 1988); Okla. Stat. tit. 58 §§ 851-897 (1965 & Supp. 1989); Or. Rev. Stat. §§ 126.100-.413 (1987); 20 Pa. Cons. Stat. Ann. §§ 5511-5525 (Purdon 1975 & Supp. 1989); R.I. Gen. Laws §§ 33-15-8 to -45 (1956 & Supp. 1988); S.C. Code Ann. §§ 62-5-101 to -624 (1976 & Supp. 1988); S.D. Codified Laws Ann. §§ 30-27-14 (1988) *vol. missing; Tenn. Code Ann. §§ 34-4-101 to -310 (1987 & Supp. 1988); Tex. Prob. Code Ann. §§ 108-127A, 130A-1300 (Vernon 1980 & Supp. 1989); (Utah Code Ann. §§ 75-5-303(2)); Vt. Stat. Ann. tit. 14 §§ 2671-3044 (1982 & Supp. 1988); Va. Code Ann. §§ 37.1-128.01 to .147 (1987 & Supp. 1988); Wash. Rev. Code Ann. §§ 11.88.005-.150, 92.010-.190 (1987 & Supp. 1989); W. Va. Code §§ 27-11-1 to 5 (1986 & Supp. 1988); *vol. missing (Wisc. Stat. Ann. § 880.08 (West 1983)); Wyo. Stat. §§ 3-1-101 to 3-6-119 (1988).

9. E.g., a court may have the authority to authorize termination of life sustaining treatment for an incompetent, but a guardian may not be allowed to do so absent specific judicial approval. E.g., Arkansas law requires that a guardian seek prior judicial approval to terminate life support systems. (Ark. Stat. Ann.) The Supreme Court of the State of Washington held that court intervention is required whenever there is a disagreement between pertinent parties (i.e., Doctor, guardian and family) about terminating life support systems. (*In re Hamlin*, 1984)

10. The ward and interested third parties, however, can ask the court to intervene and change the guardianship status by petitioning for removal of the guardian or restoration of competency or an accounting for assets. (Brakel et al., 1985)

11. The term "ward" refers to the adult individual for whom the court has appointed a guardian. Not every jurisdiction uses the term ward. Some describe the individual as the "incompetent" or the "incapacitated" individual. For purposes of this article, the term ward will be used. It should not be confused with minors who are considered legally incompetent because they are below the age of majority (age eighteen or twenty-one).

12. By noninstitutional guardians is meant individuals who act as guardians and are not acting on behalf of an institution such as a bank, governmental agency or nonprofit organization. The evaluation of these institutional actors presents another set of difficulties.

13. For example, the Pennsylvania Older Adults Protective Services Act defines "exploitation," inter alia, as an act that ". . . results in monetary personal or other benefit, gain or profit for the perpetrator or monetary or personal loss to the older adult." Of Sam's activities, some seem to fall within the letter (if not the intent) of the law.

14. An examination of every state guardianship statute did not yield any evidence that guardians are held to a special standard of care, nor has any case law been found on the subject.

15. The court could only have the power to fine and not imprison. The guardianship law could provide that guardian mistreatment of a ward is a criminal act. But that would not allow the appointing court to penalize the guardian. The local district attorney would have to file criminal charges against the guardian. In effect, this would essentially duplicate the criminal punishment available under the state protection from abuse act.

16. The most persuasive evidence of need for the training of guardians would be proof that guardians abuse and neglect their wards or that guardians do not know how to handle their responsibilities. Such proof would only be possible by an in-depth examination of the performance of guardians by qualified researchers. Even if researchers do not discover whether guardians abuse and neglect their ward, they will probably discover, due to lack of training and supervision, that the performance of guardians could be much improved.

17. States which do require periodic reporting by the guardian include e.g., Cal. Prob. Code § 1850(a) (Deering 1981 & Supp. 1989); Mich. Comp. Laws Ann. § 330.1631(2) (West 1988 & Supp. 1989); Nev. Rev. Stat. Ann. § 159.081(1) (Michie 1986 & Supp. 1988).

18. E.g., Ariz. Rev. Stat. Ann. §§ 14-5301 to 5314 (1988 & Supp. 1989); Cal. Prob. Code §§ 1500-1601, 1800-1910, 2100-2808 (Deering 1981 & Supp. 1989); Ill. Ann. Stat. ch. 110 1/2, para. 13-1 to -5 (Smith-Hurd 1988 & Supp. 1989).

19. I would not even attempt to guess how many wards that a visitor could visit and report upon in a year. The actual number is irrelevant for purposes of this article, but it would be a number worth knowing if the use of visitors is going to be successfully sold to the legislature.

20. The practice of charging the estates of incompetent individuals for the cost of state supplied services is fairly common. Pennsylvania, for example, charges the cost of state hospitals for the mentally ill to the residents until it depletes their assets. Once impoverished, the resident qualifies for Medicaid which pays for the institutionalized cost of the individual.

REFERENCES

Ark. Stat. Ann. 28-65-302 (1987 & Supp. 1988).

Brakel, S., Parry, J., & Weiner, B., (Eds.) (1985). *The mentally disabled and the law* (p. 370) Chicago: American Bar Foundation.

Faulkner, L.R. (1982). Mandating the reporting of suspected elder abuse: An inappropriate, ineffective & ageist response to the abuse of older adults. *Family Law Quarterly*, *16*, 73-74.

In re Hamlin, 689 P.2d 1372 (Wash. 1984).

Katz, K.D. (1980). Elder abuse. *Journal of Family Law*, *18*, 711.

Note (1986). Mandatory reporting of elder abuse: A cheap but ineffective solution to the problem, *Fordham Urban L.J.*, *XIV*, 723.

Pepper (Sept.25, 1987). "Abuses in guardianship of the elderly and infirm: A national disgrace," Testimony before Sub-Committee on Health and Long-Term Care House Select Committee on Aging.

Steinmetz, S. (1988). *Elder abuse and family care*, pp. 564-573. Sage.

U.S. Congress Select Committee on Aging (1985). *Elder abuse: A national disgrace* (Comm. Pub. No. 99-502) Washington, D.C., U.S. Government Printing Office.

Van den Haag, E. (1981). Punishment as a device for controlling the crime rate. *Rutgers L. Rev*, *33*, 706.

Uses of Guardianship as a Protective Intervention for Frail, Older Adults

Madelyn Anne Iris, PhD

SUMMARY. The uses of guardianship as a protective intervention for frail, older adults, especially those at risk for abuse and exploitation, are examined. Findings are based on results from four projects: a model project providing guardianship services to low-income older adults; an elder abuse demonstration project; a study of judicial decisionmaking on guardianship and the elderly; and a survey of guardianship petitions and adjudications. The findings suggest that guardianship is not always the most effective means for meeting the needs of at-risk older adults, and guardianships do sometimes fail to protect wards from abuse and neglect. Eight recommendations for developing guardianship alternative programs are offered.

INTRODUCTION

Projections on the growth of the elderly segment of the U.S. population, and the implications of this rise for American society as a whole, frequently referred to as the "demographic imperative," make it clear that the need for protections for the frail and vulnerable elderly will continue to grow throughout the rest of this century

---

Madelyn Anne Iris is Assistant Director of Education at the Center on Aging at Northwestern University, McGaw Medical Center, 750 N. Lake Shore Drive, Suite 521, Chicago, IL 60611.

Support for the projects described in this article was received from The Retirement Research Foundation, The Chicago Community Trust, the Field Foundation, United Way of Chicago, the Suburban Area Agency on Aging, and the Illinois Department on Aging.

and into the next. One aspect of this need is the provision of financial and legal protections.

Guardianship is perhaps the most common, best known, and most studied of all legal protective services used to aid older adults. In the last three to five years there has been increasing examination of guardianship for the elderly, particularly with a focus on abuse and exploitation (Associated Press, 1987; ABA Commission on Legal Problems of the Elderly, 1989). Legislative interest at the national level resulted in special subcommittee hearings as well as the introduction of several bills aimed at guardianship reform (H.R. 5266 and H.R. 372).

References to older adults as "frail" or "impaired" frequently found in guardianship studies apply to individuals who share the two major characteristics of older age and impaired decisionmaking. However, within this class we find a high degree of diversity and need. For example, the descriptors apply to individuals who, prior to the onset of debilitating age-associated diseases, functioned independently and lived an autonomous lifestyle. Now beset by conditions such as Alzheimer's disease, multi-infarct dementias, Parkinson's Disease or even late-onset depressions, they have become unable to subsist without a high degree of assistance and supervision. Many of these individuals have attentive family members willing to take on the tasks associated with a guardianship and committed to providing life-long care and support.

However, other older adults may have long histories of impairment. Many people suffering from a chronic mental illness come to the attention of the protective service system only as they age. For many of these individuals, especially those who never married, old age mirrors the aging of their entire support system, including siblings and other relatives. Hence the inability of a caring spouse to continue to provide the support and supervision needed by a mentally ill husband or wife may provoke a set of circumstances culminating in the imposition of a guardianship.

In other examples a trauma such as stroke or brain injury from a fall may be a cause for pursuing guardianship, especially if consent for medical treatment is an issue. Yet frequently the family itself may be ill-prepared to deal with the sudden onset of a relative's incapacity, and, in several examples, those family members now expected to act as decisionmakers and care providers have themselves always been dependent on the now-debilitated older person.

It is important to understand this diversity and its implications for the guardianship system, for it emphasizes the need to apply guardianships on an individual basis; both in terms of scope of power as well as length of time of imposition. Guardianships ought not to be viewed as a singular "cure" for the wide variety of symptoms displayed by those elderly individuals whose incapacities affected their decisionmaking abilities.

Our understanding of the application of guardianship to these diverse sub-populations has been hampered by a piecemeal approach to research, a dearth of evaluation studies, and an overall lack of knowledge about how guardianship actually serves older people. No national research focusing specifically on guardianship and the elderly exists, and no broad-based studies of implementation of guardianship reforms have been undertaken. Existing surveys of guardianship systems rely primarily on reports by court personnel rather than systematic and rigorous data collection. For example, in 1986 the American Bar Association's Commission on Legal Problems of the Elderly conducted a self-reporting survey of court systems focusing on a limited number of guardianship issues, particularly due process issues. Responses tended to be based on recollections and impressions rather than statistical analyses of court records. Recent studies of court systems and guardianship have been narrowly drawn, and limited to local or state agencies or systems (Friedman and Savage, 1988; Iris, 1986a, 1986b, 1989; Legal Services for the Elderly, Inc., 1985; Peters, Schmidt, and Miller, 1985; and Wilbur, 1988).

In Illinois, social service providers and researchers in the metropolitan Chicago area have been examining various aspects of the state's guardianship system and its use for older adults since 1982. This paper describes findings from four different studies of guardianship and the elderly and makes recommendations regarding the application of this protective service to the frail elderly at risk of abuse and exploitation.

BACKGROUND

Illinois law on guardianships for disabled adults was radically amended in 1979 to incorporate what were then considered to be significant and comprehensive amendments to the Guardianship for Disabled Adults Act (Ill. Rev. Stat. ch. 110 1/2). These amendments included a number of provisions aimed at expanding due process protections, enhancing the use of the least restrictive protections through limited guardianships, and streamlining estate management while encouraging the involvement of the ward and his or her family in the planning process (Jost, 1980). Three of the four projects described below were developed in response to these changes, while the fourth was designed to examine the characteristics of elder abuse and the use of legal interventions in dealing with this particular problem.

FINDINGS

The Model Project of Guardianship for the Low-Income Aged (the guardianship project) was a joint project involving six voluntary social service agencies and the Metropolitan Chicago Coalition on Aging. Between July, 1982 and June, 1985 the Guardianship Project provided guardianship and other protective services to 45 clients, through a collaborative model of service provision and consultation (Grossman, 1985; Iris, 1986a). Guardianship project clients ranged in age from 59 to 95 years, with a median age of 80. Eighty per cent were women and most were widowed. Sixty-seven per cent of the clients were white. All lived within the greater metropolitan Chicago area.

Despite the fact that guardianship is frequently perceived as an intervention which is most effective in dealing with money management and estate issues, the guardianship project was specifically designed to serve the low-income elderly. Thus, although some apparently indigent clients did in fact hold substantial assets, most were living at or below poverty level. Actual income levels at the time of referral were low: the median income, excluding assets, was only $365.00 a month. Many clients were either already on Supplemental Security Income or were eligible for this benefit. For most clients, referral to the guardianship project was precipitated by a perceived escalation of risk coupled with increased problems in coping (Grossman 1985:10-12).

Through a tri-partite committee structure comprised of representatives from the six participating agencies, the project examined a wide range of policy and practice questions emerging from the provision of guardianship services to 23 elderly clients. Financial payee services were offered to 13 clients and protective services of a non-legal nature were recommended for another 9 clients. In addition to the 45 clients actually referred for guardianship review to the project, forty more were screened for referral at the individual agencies but were not brought to the project for review, as guardianship was not deemed to be the most effective intervention. Thus, guardianship was determined to be appropriate for only a limited segment of the project's potential clients and for those with particular types of problems. Overall, agency staff believed they could intervene and achieve a satisfactory resolution in over 70% of the protective service cases without resorting to a legal intervention as drastic as guardianship.

While the project did not specifically examine the role of abuse and neglect in provoking the need for a guardianship, Grossman reports that in three cases the caretaker was reported to be financially exploiting the older person and in one of these cases physical abuse was reported as well. Guardianship was used to resolve these situations although more abuse was reported among the thirteen clients who received payeeship services. These included three cases in which financial exploitation was reported and one of financial exploitation as well as emotional abuse. These four cases constitute 31% of all payeeship cases.

Clients who received guardianship services tended to live in more threatening or unsafe situations than those who received payeeships or other non-legal protective services. Thus, it would appear that one function of a guardianship is to ensure safer and better living conditions for the ward. However, in contrast, physical health problems were greatest for those clients who received non-legal support services and who were not referred for guardianship. This suggests that clients' health problems could be effectively dealt with outside of the guardianship system, or, they could not be dealt with at all. As Grossman notes, ". . . when major client problems were related to the client's refusal to seek medical care, guardianship was not a useful intervention . . ." (1985:17).

The ethical issues related to protective service provision to resistant clients suspected of suffering from impaired decisionmaking are highly charged and generated much debate at project meetings. Questions such as agency liability, client autonomy, and client advocacy were raised, as was the more philosophical question of what is an appropriate role for a voluntary social service agency vis-à-vis clients in need of protective services. These were discussed further in a series of three roundtables sponsored by the Metropolitan Chicago Coalition on Aging during 1986 (MCCoA, 1986), which brought together members of the original policy committee of the guardianship project as well as attorneys, judges, and representatives from several state agencies and local area agencies on aging.

In examining the question of the appropriateness of guardianship as a protective intervention, the project's most outstanding finding was that guardianship was not always the best or most effective intervention for meeting the needs of the frail elderly. The figures cited above indicate that in almost half the cases, from a social services perspective which emphasizes client autonomy and use of the least restrictive intervention, guardianship was not always the service of choice, especially when dealing with abuse and neglect. This may be so because of particular statutory restrictions on the guardian's power which led agency participants to believe that even a guardianship would not serve to aid the client.

Cases of self neglect highlight this finding. Illinois law does not authorize guardians to remove an individual from her home against her will, nor does a guardian have the power to sign a ward into a psychiatric facility (the most recent Illinois Governor's Commission to Revise the Mental Health Code (1988) has recommended that the Illinois statute be amended to offer guardians this power. No action has been taken on this recommendation). Thus, workers believed that a guardianship would not necessarily remedy a situation in which the client was refusing to leave a clearly substandard and dangerous dwelling nor would a guardianship ensure that those elderly who were refusing treatment due to psychiatric disorders would obtain medical and psychiatric care.

In contrast, guardianships were effective in protecting frail elders from abusive caretakers or relatives, when decisionmaking capacity was clearly impaired. However, in most of these cases the ward was subsequently placed in a nursing home. Since the intent of the project was to use guardianship as a tool for maintaining wards in the community, institutionalization was not perceived as a positive outcome.

Additional information on the use of guardianship as a tool of intervention in cases of elder abuse and neglect was gathered from a two year elder abuse demonstration project conducted by the Metropolitan Chicago Coalition on Aging as one component of the North Suburban Cook County Elder Abuse Project. This project was one of four demonstration projects in Illinois funded from 1985-1987 (Hwalek, Hill, and Stahl, 1989; Iris, 1987; Segal and Iris, 1989). The North Suburban project served approximately 236 clients over a 27 month period and provided assessment, intervention, and follow-up services (Iris, 1987 and Hwalek, 1988).

Demographic findings of the elder abuse project concur with those of other researchers: approximately three fourths of the clients were women, and over 50% were 75 years of age or older. In fact, less than 10% of the clients were between the ages of 60 and 64. Sixty-one per cent of the clients lived in their own homes, and most lived with a spouse or child.

Although the project was designed to emphasize the use of legal interventions such as orders of protection and guardianship, the findings demonstrate that neither tool was perceived as the most appropriate intervention for resolving elder abuse, at least for the population served by this project. State findings (Hwalek, 1988) indicate that although workers assessed approximately 29% of the elder abuse clients as disoriented, only about seven out of 307 had any type of guardian at the time of referral and only one client out of 557 was identified as having a guardian of the estate. Only 4% of the clients had powers of attorney established. In suburban Cook County guardianships were recommended for fewer than 10% of the clients although in several additional cases family members were said to be considering a guardianship through private means.

Interpretation of the infrequent usage of guardianship as a tool for resolving cases of elder abuse and neglect in the face of high rates of confusion and disorientation is complicated. In particular, since no standards for assessing confusion, disorientation, and lack of decisionmaking capacity were established as guidelines for use by investigators, it is difficult to determine the real import of these figures and the need for guardianship. Many times, in fact, workers commented that they described a client as having poor judgement and decisionmaking abilities just because she was not extricating herself from an abusive or exploitative situation. True cases of decisional impairment cannot be discerned from the existing data.

Yet, although few clients were judged impaired enough to require the protection of a guardianship, a client's inability to adequately protect her assets from exploitation was a significant cause of referral for elder abuse services. Financial exploitation occurred in just over 33% of the cases. The most common type of abuse was the category "other," which included verbal abuse and harassment. Abuse of this sort was reported in almost half of all cases. Physical abuse was almost as common. Deprivation and neglect together occurred in over 40% of the cases, while self-neglect was reported in 16% of the referrals. More than one type of abuse was indicated in over half the cases reported. The high rate of financial exploitation and the rather significant number of cases of self-neglect suggest that some mechanisms for protecting older adults from abuse and neglect are required, even if such persons are not incapacitated to the extent that guardianship is clearly required.

To better understand the judicial perspective on guardianship, an ethnographic study of judicial decisionmaking was undertaken in 1986, to explicate the process used by judges in making determinations of incapacity (Iris, 1986b). Findings from this study indicate that guardianships are used for a wide variety of reasons, including estate management, consent for nursing home placement and consent for medical treatment. In outlining precipitating causes for guardianships, judges rarely described cases involving abuse or neglect by others. Instead, they focused on situations in which the elderly person's impairments led directly to mismanagement of funds or the inability to even acknowledge an estate. Many other cases involved consent for medical treatment for elderly individuals with psychiatric disorders or mental disabilities which prevented them from seeking appropriate medical treatment for either physical or mental illnesses.

Since actual or potential cases of abuse and neglect were not issues of concern for the judges, it is difficult to determine the incidence of such occurrences in guardianship cases, either at the time of petitioning or later. Court room observations led to the conclusion that when petitions for guardianship were contested, or when an existing guardianship was protested, most often the contest grew out of conflicts among relatives over who should be the guardian or how an estate was managed, not over the need for the guardianship itself.

Allegations of abuse, neglect and financial exploitation were not uncommon. Yet, in this limited sample of contested or challenged cases, judges did not specifically respond to these charges by taking some type of investigatory action, such as directing a guardian ad litem to make an independent inquiry. No examples were noted in which family members were ordered to resolve their differences through formal mediation processes or through family counseling. [In a personal communication one judge has reported using these alternatives more and more frequently as a preferred method for dealing with family conflicts around guardianships. No formal documentation on this use exists.]

To enhance these findings and to provide a context in which to evaluate them, the author undertook a survey of guardianships opened in 1985 in three Illinois counties: Cook, Lake and DuPage (Iris, 1989). This survey had several purposes: to establish a data base on guardianship, as a baseline for future survey research, and to establish a concrete data base for assessing the reliability of the findings of earlier research. Findings from this survey reveal that guardianship is a system which affects older adults more than any other group of people: for example, in Cook County the median age of respondents (those named in a petition for guardianship) was 72. Sixty-six per cent of the total sample were over sixty years of age and of these, 47% were 80 or older. These findings are comparable to those in Lake and DuPage counties. As might be expected, given the high median age, 60% of the sample was female, although this percentage varied with age. In fact, slightly over half the respondents in the younger age ranges were men.

In Cook County, the majority of guardianships awarded to older adults were plenary guardianships of both estate and person. In all, 53% of all guardianships awarded in 1985 were of this type, but for older adults, these full guardianships were awarded 67% of the time. Temporary guardianships for the purpose of placement in nursing homes and consent for medical treatment were very common. Some form of temporary guardianship was awarded in approximately 20% of the cases, and the majority of these were for the purpose of placing the ward in a nursing home or consenting to medical treatment. Almost all (88.4%) were awarded to older adults. Finally, in all three counties the number of people restored to competency or awarded limited or less restrictive types of guardianships than plenary, was almost nil. Few petitions for guardianship were dismissed for causes other than the death of the respondent prior to the guardianship hearing.

Although data was collected on guardianship cases involving alleged or substantiated abuse and neglect, the incidence of such cases appears to be very low. However, it is clear from the types of reports found in the files, and from discussions with members of the judiciary and service providing agencies, that abuse and neglect by guardians or others is not a major concern to those providing protective services to the frail elderly. Case study information suggests that indicators of possible abuse frequently go ignored by both guardians ad litem (attorneys appointed prior to adjudication to investigate the facts of the petition), as well as court personnel.

For example, in one case, letters from a family member alleging abuse by the guardian were forwarded by the court to the guardian's lawyer and no evidence of further action was found in the file. In another instance, the guardian of the estate, a bank, was so remiss in paying the ward's rent, she was eventually evicted. No action was initiated by the court to either sanction the guardian of the estate or to order its removal. In other examples respondents made clear statements to the court investigators that they did not want the petitioner named guardian, yet no detailed inquiries into the facts underlying such statements were documented. Possible abuse by the petitioner was not considered and in most examples the petitioner was appointed guardian.

DISCUSSION

The findings described above provide a mixed view of the use of guardianship as a protective intervention in cases of abuse and neglect for older adults. The perception of guardianship as the most restrictive intervention was substantiated as data show that guardianship must be considered irreversible, ending only with death. In addition, the court consistently imposes the greatest degree of intervention, despite options for less restrictive alternatives such as limited guardianships.

The specter of guardianship abuses raised by reports such as that of the Associated Press (1987), cannot be dismissed as simply an aberration or isolated incident. As the docket survey and other research described above reveal, questions of abuse and exploitation by guardians remain unanswered. Abuse by a guardian was a very infrequent occurrence in the elder abuse project, and guardianship itself played only a minor role in the typical scenario of abuse and neglect of an elderly person. Similarly, abuse by guardians was not perceived as a significant problem by the courts, nor were many examples of abuse or neglect by guardians documented in the court records. However, these findings ought not to be construed as evidencing lack of occurrence, but rather suggest that greater awareness of the potential problems of abuse must be generated within the court system.

In addition, there are numerous examples in which the court fails to properly monitor the guardian of the estate, and in Illinois, guardians of the person are not monitored at all. Instead, the court relies on intervention by interested parties to bring abuses and improprieties to its attention. Since many older adults with guardians are either living in nursing homes or are homebound, it is not likely that community interest will serve to protect them from abuse and exploitation.

Susceptibility to abuse and neglect is heightened since self-advocacy by wards is very difficult. The imposition of a guardianship makes it almost impossible for a ward to secure the services of an attorney independently. Thus, even if capable, it is extremely difficult for an individual under a guardianship to take action on his or her own behalf. Furthermore, since guardians also have the ability to restrict the ward's movements and to place a ward in an institutional setting which limits her ability to interact with individuals other than those that represent the facility itself, it is unlikely that the ward herself will be able to access existing advocacy systems.

In cases of self-neglect, statutory restrictions give guardianship a questionable utility since those services most needed, i.e., relocation and medical care, are not easily attainable even with a guardian. In clearly defined cases of elder abuse and neglect, guardianships appear to be used infrequently, since most persons characterized as victims of elder abuse and neglect are not so impaired that they require the imposition of a guardian.

A complicating factor in elder abuse is the fact that most abuse of the elderly occurring outside of an institutional setting is perpetuated by a close family member (Iris, 1987; Hwalek, 1988; Steinmetz, 1988). When family members are inappropriate, it is often difficult to find someone willing and able to petition for guardianship and/or serve as the guardian. Although Illinois has a state guardian mandated to provide guardianship services to persons with low incomes and assets, at the time of these studies this office was not filing petitions to initiate guardianships. Resources for this service had to be found elsewhere. The protective service specialist at the Chicago area agency on aging reports that this remains a major barrier to the provision of appropriate protective services for the abused elderly (Melcher, personal communication). Were petitioning services available, this office would seek guardianships on a regular basis. However, no elder abuse data from this office has been examined to substantiate this conclusion.

CONCLUSION

These statements are intended to raise our awareness of the pitfalls of the system, and keep us from viewing guardianship as a final solution to the problem of how to best assist the frail elderly and the disabled. Findings from the various projects described here demonstrate that guardianship appears to have only limited potential in enhancing the delivery of protective services to frail elderly suffering from abuse and neglect.

With this in mind, we should be prepared to consider the need for continued emphasis on the development of guardianship alternatives programs, as these appear to offer more viable means of intervention in cases of abuse and neglect, including self-neglect. A number of conditions are offered as guidelines for planning a guardianship diversion or guardianship alternatives program:

1. Incapacity or incompetency is not always clear. Decisional capacity may vary, relative to a number of factors. These include but are not limited to: (1) the effects of medication; (2) time of day; (3) nutritional status; (4) orientation to a new environment; (5) loss of orientation in a restricted environment such as a hospital; (6) confusion and depression due to illness; and (7) depression and withdrawal due to loss. Since guardianships are almost impossible to overturn, one should seek other alternatives if any of these factors might be affecting the decisionmaking ability of an individual.

2. When a guardianship is sought to achieve a single purpose, such as discharge to a nursing home, some other alternative, less restrictive in its implications, ought to be considered. If no such alternative exists, legislation or statutory changes ought to be considered and pursued.

3. If the guardianship will have no long-term benefit to the ward, some other alternative must be sought, again, because a guardianship "is forever."

4. If the goal is to preserve personal autonomy, some mechanism other than guardianship should be sought to provide the needed safeguards and protections. Guardianship rarely serves this function and should not be considered as a means to this end.

5. Guardianships should not be sought when a disabling condition is considered to be curable, reversible, or transitory.

6. Guardianships should not be used to resolve conflicts regarding estate management or custody and care of an impaired person. Guardianship alternative projects should include a component for referral to mediation and dispute resolution services to aid in such cases.

7. Individuals who are victims of abuse and neglect must be carefully assessed to determine whether or not decisionmaking incapacity is a real factor in the abuse situation. Guardianships should not be sought solely as a means for removing the victim from an abusive situation, especially when the abuse occurs within the home of

the victim. Alternatives such as orders of protection and involuntary commitments for the abuser must be considered even though they may be more difficult to obtain.

8. Everyone, regardless of age, has the right to live with risk. The inability to make decisions should not be confused with bad decisionmaking, nor should unitary standards of behavior be imposed. Incapacity should not be confused with eccentricity or bad choices. In addition, personal history and values plays an important role in assessing an individual's incapacity. Finally, ethnic, cultural and social class differences must also be evaluated before determining that real incapacity exists.

In considering the purpose of guardianship in the first place to protect those who cannot protect themselves, we must strive to create a system where failure cannot occur, a system with not one, but multiple safeguards. Currently, we are far from having such a system.

REFERENCES

American Bar Association. (1986). *Statement of recommended judicial practices. Commission on Legal Problems of the Elderly*, American Bar Association, Washington, D.C.

American Bar Association. (1989). *Guardianship: An agenda for reform*. Commission on the Mentally Disabled, Commission on Legal Problems of the Elderly, The American Bar Association, Washington, D.C.

Associated Press. (1987). Guardians of the elderly: An ailing system.

Friedman, L. & Savage, M. (1988). Taking care: the law of conservatorship in California. *Southern California Law Review*, *61*, 273-290.

Grossman, S. (1985). *Client data report: Model project of guardianship for the low-income aged*. Metropolitan Chicago Coalition on Aging, Chicago, IL.

Hwalek, M. (1988). *Elder abuse: The Illinois Department on Aging's final report on the elder abuse demonstration program act*. Springfield, IL, The Illinois Department on Aging.

Hwalek, M., Hill, B. & Stahl, C. (1989). The Illinois plan for a statewide elder abuse program. In R. Filenson & S. R. Ingman (Eds.), *Elder Abuse: Practice and Policy* (pp. 196-297). New York, Human Sciences Press, Inc.

Iris, M. (1986a). *Model project of guardianship for the low-income aged: Impact evaluation*. (Final Report). The Erikson Institute, Chicago, IL.

Iris, M. (1986b). *The use of limited guardianship as the least restrictive alternative for the impaired elderly: An ethnographic examination of the probate court and the decisiomaking process*. (Final Report). The Erikson Institute, Chicago, IL.

Iris, M. (1987). *The north suburban Cook County elder abuse project*. (Final Report). The Metropolitan Chicago Coalition on Aging, Chicago, IL.

Iris, M. (1989). *Implementation of the disabled adults statute in Illinois: A survey and analysis of the 1985 docket and court records in Cook, Lake and DuPage counties*. (Final Report) Metropolitan Chicago Coalition on Aging, Chicago, IL.

Jost, T. (1980). The Illinois guardianship for disabled adults legislation of 1978 and 1979: Protecting the disabled from their zealous protectors. *Chicago Kent Law Review*, *56*, 1087-1105.

Legal Services for the Elderly. (1985). *Guardianship and conservatorship practices in Maine's counties*. Legal Services for the Elderly, Washington, D.C.

Metropolitan Chicago Coalition on Aging. (1986). *The frail elderly in Illinois: Toward a protective service system*. Metropolitan Chicago Coalition on Aging, Chicago, IL.

Peters, R., Schmidt, W.C., & Miller, K.S. (1985). Guardianship of the elderly in Tallahassee, Florida. *The Gerontologist*, *25*, 532-538.

Segal, S. & Iris, M.A. (1989). Strategies for service provision: The use of legal interventions in a systems approach to casework. In R. Filenson & S. R. Ingman (Eds.), *Elder Abuse: Practice and Policy* (pp. 104-116). New York, Human Sciences Press, Inc.

Steinmetz, S. (1988). *Duty bound: Elder abuse and family care*. Newbury Park, CA: Sage Publications.

A Judicial Menu: Selecting Remedies for the Incapacitated Elder

Bobbe Shapiro Nolan, BSN, JD

SUMMARY. An "incapacitated" elderly person may be brought to probate court in proceedings to impose adult protective services, involuntary commitment for mental illness, or guardianship. If the person or agency bringing the petition has chosen a remedy the criteria of which do not fit the respondent, the case is likely to be dismissed without assuring assistance to the elderly person. Suggesting that judges take a global view, the article encourages them to ask, "What remedy is appropriate for this person, in this situation?" Key to choosing the remedy is comprehensive, functional evaluation of the respondent by a qualified human services professional. The article discusses content of the evaluation, available resources, and implications of the judicial menu approach for the respondent and the court.

The 83-year-old "respondent" appears in the courtroom without counsel on a hot July day. Emma Lyons is skinny and not very clean, but has evidently made some effort to groom herself for the hearing. A heavy coat partially hides food spots on her orange sweater and blue and green print skirt. Her stockings sag around swollen, reddened ankles, and the red tennis shoes have holes cut to relieve pressure on bunions. Deaf, senile, psychotic, or simply rude, she interrupts the judge, the bailiff, and the opposing attorney with irrelevant and repetitious comments: "They all lie, you know. It's a violation of my rights. That girl came into my house and just took things. And she wants my cats. They're show quality, you

---

Bobbe Shapiro Nolan is Executive Director of the Wilmington Senior Center, Inc., 1901 Market Street, Wilmington, DE 19802.

know, they're valuable." "I have to keep those things, judge, you know, all my papers. You have to have papers to prove your Social Security. They come and take it away from you."

There is testimony. Her house has been condemned: no running water; countless vermin; "approximately" 58 cats; five rooms filled with stacks of newspaper, bags of garbage, and mounds of used clothing; a refrigerator crammed with putrescent vegetables and meat scraps intended for her pets. She screams at neighborhood children, who regard her as a witch. She wanders around muttering to unseen persons: her mother, her daughter. And yet—her bank account is in perfect order. She has never missed a house payment; there are no bills in arrears. On her walls are certificates of appreciation for past civic involvement and charitable donations. She drives her immaculate old Cadillac to church each week. A retired teacher, she writes cogent letters to the editor on public and religious affairs.

It is a guardianship hearing. In this state, if guardianship is imposed, Emma Lyons will lose the right to control her money, decide on her place of residence, retain her teaching certificate, vote, drive a car, or make a valid contract. She has refused assistance from caseworkers from Adult Protective Services, and rejects any suggestion of mental health intervention.

You are the judge.

* * *

Every year, judges and human services providers in every county in the United States are confronted by people like Emma Lyons. Someone—family, neighbors, an agency—cares enough to try to impose assistance on neglected, resistive, troublesome elders. What form should that assistance take? Is one alternative more restrictive than another for this woman? Who should decide the appropriate remedy for her difficulties?

Consistent with our legal tradition, someone filed a petition for Emma's guardianship. In effect, the person filing the petition decided that guardianship would be the best remedy for Emma. The judge will decide whether or not she fits the criteria for incompetence or incapacity in that state, and whether a guardian will be appointed for her. If he denies the petition, Emma is left without help, angry and triumphant. But, what if the judge answered a different question? what if, instead of asking, "Is this an incompetent or incapacitated person for whom a guardian must be appointed?" the judge asked, "What kind of protection is most appropriate for this cat-loving 83-year-old widow who manages her finances adequately, but neglects her personal care?" To workers in human services, this is the logical question. They become frustrated and upset when, after all their efforts to lay the groundwork for a guardianship case (or a protective services case, or a mental illness commitment) the petition is dismissed. They have no recourse. The lawyers walk away. In traditional jurisprudence, everyone has done his job.

SCOPE

This paper suggests that courts consider the full range of state-authorized remedies in these cases, applying the remedy appropriate to the respondent's situation, regardless of the nature of the petition. The remedies—imposition of involuntary adult protective services, commitment for mental illness, and partial or plenary guardianship—fall within the jurisdiction of probate or chancery courts. Because all derive from the traditional equitable jurisdiction of such courts (although adult protective services and partial guardianship are statutory variations on equitable themes), this departure from the petition-specific analysis should pose few conceptual problems. Rather, the approach raises questions about the nature of proper notice to respondents, judicial discomfort with a diagnostic/therapeutic interpretation of the court's role, and the potentially repressive nature of a plenary protective view.

The paper does not discuss the more basic philosophical question of whether, or when, government should have the right to intervene in the life of the self-neglecting, impaired elder. By the time these individuals appear in court, some person or agency has already decided that the situation poses sufficient danger to the individual or to society to warrant intervention, and the respondent has already refused to comply voluntarily. Nor does the paper deal broadly with the topic of guardianship reform. Many recent recommendations for reform of the guardianship system have great merit. The reader is particularly referred to the American Bar Association's *Guardianship: An Agenda for Reform* (1989) and the National Conference of the Judiciary on Guardianship Proceedings for the Elderly's *Statement of Recommended Judicial Practices* (1986).

THE RANGE OF REMEDIES

The three remedies available (with assorted variations) to probate judges are familiar to readers of this publication. It is tempting to regard imposition of adult protective services, mental illness commitment, and guardianship as steps on a continuum of least restrictive alternatives for care in the assumed mental deterioration of the elderly. Such a concept is misleading, however; each remedy can be exceedingly repressive. For example, once protective services are imposed, the respondent can be involuntarily removed from his home and placed in a nursing or boarding home, his pets and other nuisance property can be removed and destroyed, and he can be required to pay for all this. The same person, if found to be mentally ill, might enjoy greater legal protection of his property interests, but could be involuntarily medicated or physically restrained and confined behind locked doors. At least one court has held that involuntary commitment is more restrictive than guardianship (*In re Boyer*, 1981). If a guardian is appointed, the respondent's right to choose his dwelling place and to consent to or refuse medical treatment are often subject to the guardian's interpretation of what is in his best interests, without any recourse easily available to the ward. The incompetent ward usually is deprived of driver's and other licenses by the imposition for the guardianship.

Each of the remedies has its own set of definitions, procedures, and restrictions. In the paragraphs below, we will discuss the imposition of each remedy in a general overview. Of course, each state's law should be consulted to determine specific procedural requirements.

Adult Protective Services

Adult protective services statutes have been passed in many states to provide a community-based mechanism for investigating and protecting the elderly from abuse, neglect, and exploitation. The statutes usually require various classes of professionals to report instances of suspected abuse, neglect or exploitation to a county welfare or human services department or to a centralized state telephone hotline. Other individuals may report suspected cases to the same authority; civil and criminal immunity for those making a complaint in good faith are assured by the statute. Authorized investigation of the allegations takes place within a prescribed time. Investigators – usually county social workers – are required to see and speak with the person at-risk at his residence, consult with the person who made the report, and file a written report with the state. If anyone interferes with the investigation, the county welfare department may seek a court order for access to the alleged victim. Various social, medical, and assistive services may be provided to the consenting at-risk adult until he is deemed to be at risk no longer.

If the adult refuses services or resists the investigation, and the investigator believes an emergency exists, the welfare department may seek court authorization to impose protective services on the adult. This petition must include an allegation that the person is "incapacitated" – unable to make or carry out reasonable decisions in daily living that facilitate the provision of food, shelter, clothing, and health care necessary for life support, with or without the help of a caregiver. There are various notice, representation, and hearing rights; if the adult is found to be incapacitated, protective services will be imposed. These services may include placement in an institution if that is found to be the least restrictive alternative available. The adult who is able to pay for protective services may be ordered to do so (*Matter of Protective Services for Hartman*, 1987).

Commitment for Mental Illness

As a result of U.S. Supreme Court decisions, guidelines for involuntary mental illness commitment are similar in most states. Someone with knowledge must allege that the respondent is dangerous to himself or others, or is so gravely disabled that he cannot provide for his basic needs and would benefit from hospitalization for his mental illness. Absent an emergency, someone must file an affidavit documenting mental illness and dangerous behavior; usually the signature of a psychiatrist, psychologist, and/or licensed physician is required. (As a practical matter, the physician will often be required to arrange for a bed at the receiving institution.) If the court orders prehearing detention, the respondent can be transported by authorized personnel immediately (or within a brief time); he will be notified of the reasons for his confinement either just before or soon after being transported. A notification of general, legal, and treatment rights should be provided soon after arrival. A hearing, usually conducted by a judge or court referee at the hospital, follows the confinement of the respondent within a prescribed time. The respondent may choose an attorney, or have one appointed by the court (Van Duizend, McGraw & Keilitz, 1984).

Guardianship

Innumerable reviews of the guardianship process in all its variations are available. Briefly, a petition for guardianship must allege some grounds for a finding of incompetence or incapacity. (For a review of the various grounds and their relationship to functional evaluation, readers are referred to this author's previous publication (1984).) Most states now require personal service of the notice on the putative ward, provide for a hearing, and permit legal representation; some states will appoint an attorney or guardian *ad litem* if the ward is unrepresented. If a guardian is appointed, the ward loses many legal rights, including the right to execute a valid contract, marry, hold a license, consent to medical care, vote, and to control his finances and the circumstances under which he lives.

Because plenary guardianship can be so restrictive, many states have developed mechanisms to impose partial, limited, or reviewable guardianships. Even in those states where plenary guardianship is the norm, courts have held that the equitable powers of probate courts include the authority to limit powers of the guardian (*Judicial Practices*, p. 45).

ONE COMMON THREAD: THE FUNCTIONAL EVALUATION

A Component of Each Remedy

Among the conditions required for imposition of each of the remedies is impaired functioning in activities of daily living. The mentally ill person subject to involuntary commitment is so gravely impaired that he cannot provide for his basic needs for food, clothing, or shelter, or is unable to provide for his own health and safety (Beis, 1983). The person subject to the involuntary imposition of adult protective services is unable to make or carry out reasonable decisions in daily living that facilitate the provision of food, shelter, clothing, and health care necessary for life support (Ohio Rev. Code Annot. Sec. 5101.60, 1981). The person for whom a guardian is appointed must lack the capacity to meet essential requirements for physical health or safety such as those actions necessary to provide the health care, food, shelter, clothing, personal hygiene, and other care without which serious physical injury or illness is more likely than not to occur (ABA Model Guardianship Statute, 1979; N.H. Rev. Stat. Ann. Sec. 464-A:2(VII, XI), 1983; *In re Boyer*, 1981). In essence, each of these statutory tests requires that the individual under scrutiny be incapable of carrying out activities of daily living at a level which does not endanger his health and safety.

This lack of capacity is an important point. Protective statutes generally do not deal with the individual who could make responsible decisions, but who chooses not to. The party seeking protective care for an endangered person should be prepared to prove that the respondent is incapacitated by some condition which prevents him from caring for himself. Harmless, eccentric or purposely idiosyncratic behavior remains protected if the laws are properly applied.

Medical evidence, in the form of a physician certificate, psychiatric examination, or letter of opinion from the respondent's doctor, is a commonly accepted (and sometimes essential) element of the protective hearing. It can be very helpful in establishing that there is some disease or condition which causes the respondent to be incapacitated. Unfortunately, court records often contain a physician's letter on the order of the one below:

> My patient, Emma Lyons, 83, has diagnoses of congestive heart failure, hypertension, mild adult-onset diabetes mellitus, and osteoporosis. Her last appointment at my office was six months ago. Because of her age-related mental deterioration, I believe Mrs. Lyons needs a guardian to provide her with the care she needs. (Richard Roe, MD)

Evidence of impaired functioning is best provided directly rather than by implication from medical diagnosis, since the range of human behavior resulting from any medical diagnosis varies widely. Frolik (1981) notes that "The decision . . . should be based upon the quality of the individual's decisions and behavior rather than on identifying the cause of the erratic decision making or behavior." After all, there are millions of people who suffer from arteriosclerosis, hypertension, diabetes, heart disease, cancer, schizophrenia, bipolar disorder, etc., who take perfectly adequate care of themselves and do not require protective care. The same can be said of age; advanced age in itself does not automatically cause a person to need a caregiver. Statistical correlations of old age and increased dependency will not necessarily apply to the individual case.

To establish the necessity for any of the protective mechanisms, a court should have access to recent functional assessment data from a qualified expert. In the following paragraphs we will discuss the content and method of the functional evaluation data by the court and by surrogate decision makers.

Content and Methodology

The evaluator meets with the subject at his residence, if possible. The evaluator should present identification and introduce herself and the purpose of the evaluation. I have found that candor at this time is well received; even very suspicious people respond when I assure them that I am here to see how well they manage day-to-day, and that the information is intended to help them to remain independent. Most subjects are well aware that something is going on, and secrecy or mendacity tends to give itself away. Very forgetful subjects don't remember the purpose of the visit anyway, and people with severely impaired reasoning will make no sense out of any explanation. Ethical considerations aside, honesty works best. As long as I can get inside, I can generally establish enough of a relationship to carry out the evaluation.

A number of instruments, frameworks, and scoring scales for functional evaluation have been developed and tested. All attempt to measure the subject's facility at carrying out activities of daily living. These instruments are particularly helpful in providing an organizational framework for the assessment visit, assuring the evaluator that she has covered the pertinent areas. However, most formal instruments are limited in their phrasing, requiring the evaluator to fit the subject's behavior into their terminology, and many do not give the subject credit for creative innovations involving help from others. For example, Lawton's useful "Scale for Instrumental Activities of Daily Living (IADL)" (1971) provides the following rating item:

Ability to Telephone

1. Operates telephone on own initiative; looks up and dials numbers, etc.
2. Dials a few well-known numbers.
3. Answers telephone but does not dial.
4. Does not use telephone at all.

How shall we score the woman who cannot see to dial (because her electricity has been turned off), but who knows the information operator very well and gets the operator to connect her with a broad variety of friends and service providers at all hours of the day or night? An individual who knows he has a deficit, but who finds a way to get that need met, should be credited with successful adaptation skills. For this reason (and for others which will appear below) functional evaluators should seriously consider submitting their reports as narrative rather than as scores from a standardized scale. Nonetheless, these scales are useful as organizational aids, to be sure that no crucial area of daily functioning is overlooked.

Important areas to be evaluated include: shopping, storing, preparing, and eating food; cleanliness of self, clothing and environment; access to transportation; health care management (including obtaining services of providers, medication management, rationale for noncompliance); financial management; environmental safety; use of socialization resources (including people and pets); use of recreational resources (including television). In each area, the evaluator seeks the following information: Does this person have the resources needed to function acceptably? How is he using the resources—can he get help to supplement his own efforts? Does he agree that resources are needed? Is he able (physically and mentally) to use the resources available? If he is able, but does not use them, why not? Is he satisfied with his life situation? Does he see any alternatives?

There is an essential difference between the functional evaluation and the more traditional diagnostic assessment performed by health care personnel. *In the functional evaluation, the emphasis is on resulting behavior, rather than pathological causation*. We record the extent to which the subject carries out activities of daily living effectively, and what innovations he utilizes to keep himself going. We do not concentrate on bizarre behavior if it is functional. For example: An elderly woman cares deeply for her many pets. She is too feeble to bury them and has no money to arrange burial. However, she does have a freezer, and a life insurance policy made out to a pet cemetery which will pay for the burials when she dies. As long as she pays the electric bill, having a freezer full of dead animals endangers no one. She should receive credit for her creative and responsible plan. Another example: An old man lives alone in his large house. A double amputee, he has not been upstairs in several years, having set up a bed in the dining room and acquired a portable commode on the ground floor. Neighbors reported that he was being exploited by the young man and woman who had moved in upstairs. During the investigation he agreed that his "guests" paid no rent, nor did they help with expenses, and that he really knew little about their background. However, they did the shopping, cooking, and laundry, and kept him company. He had no desire for further services. "I have all I need. I own the house, and it's going to my church after I die. My pension pays for food and utilities. Except for company, what else do I need? These legs aren't going to grow back, honey. Let's have a beer." Like food and clothing, companionship is often available only for a fee—in this case, living expenses. There are worse bargains.

Who Performs Functional Evaluation?

Obtaining functional evaluation data is not as difficult as one might think. Community health nurses, social workers, some occupational and physical therapists, mental health workers, and gerontological specialists have been doing this sort of evaluation for years. Faculty members in schools of nursing, social work, and gerontology may be available for consultation. There are also growing numbers of gerontological consultants, operating as private practitioners, who could be contacted. Many hospitals have instituted geriatric assessment units, where a multidisciplinary team of physician, geriatric nurse specialist or practitioner, and social workers performs a variety of tests and produces a comprehensive report of the elderly subject's current status with recommendations for treatment, environmental change, and family support. Such assessments cost between $250-$500, part of which may be covered by Medicare.

Although the skills needed for functional evaluation are shared by various human services professionals, no trans-professional certification system now exists in the United States. Individual professions (notably nursing and medicine) do certify gerontological specialists. A word of caution is in order, however: Physicians certified in geriatrics specialize in the diagnosis and care of the diseases of elderly people. Their education is usually incomplete in such areas as activities of daily living, social competence, informal support systems, and coordination of community resources. Johnson and Mezy (1989) recommend a multdisciplinary, collaborative or team approach to comprehensive functional evaluation of the elderly.

Some courts have created volunteer programs to carry out fact-finding visits with the ward and the petitioner in guardianship proceedings. Volunteers are trained in a court-sponsored program, and present their findings to the court (Judicial Practices. pp. 30-31). While it is unlikely such visitors will have the training necessary for a professional functional evaluation, these programs are a positive step toward a fuller factual basis for determinations of incompetency.

Currently, demonstration projects which include functional evaluation of respondents in guardianship cases by court-employed experts are being carried out by the Trumbull County, Ohio Probate Court and the Center for Social Gerontology in Ann Arbor, Michigan. Other probate courts employ or contract with professional court visitors, or simply refer respondents to appropriate social agencies for evaluation. Having this information presented by a representative of the court, rather than by expert witnesses for either side of the guardianship proceeding, may add weight to the findings. Certainly it would alleviate the potential for requiring the respondent to undergo repeated functional evaluations by opposing experts (Nolan, 1984).

Admissibility Concerns

The Uniform Guardianship and Protective Proceedings Act (1983) and other model guardianship statutes include provisions for evaluation of the respondent by representatives of the court. In those states that have adopted these models, there is no question that functional evaluation data are admissible in guardianship proceedings; in fact, evaluation may be mandatory. And in New Hampshire, where the requirements of the guardianship statute are explicitly functionally oriented, behavioral descriptions must be included in the petition and admitted to evidence at the hearing (N.H. Rev. Stat. Ann. 464-A, 1979). The New Hampshire Public Guardian Office, in fact, has produced an instruction manual for individual functional assessment of extended-care facility residents, with areas of day-to-day functioning specifically keyed to the requirements of the statute (Saunders & Simon, 1987).

Many states have not adopted statutory language requiring evaluation of the respondent in all of the proceedings under discussion. Nonetheless, such information should be admissible in guardianship, civil mental health commitment, and adult protective services proceedings. It is unquestionably relevant and material to the controversy, and no statute specifically excludes functional evaluation data from admission. Caselaw encourages fact finding of this sort, provided by experts, or by direct observation of the court.

USING A JUDICIAL MENU: PROCEDURES AND LIMITATIONS

Procedure

An overview of procedure is provided in the second section above. For each of the remedies, a petition is filed (presumably for whatever remedy the petitioner or his counsel thinks appropriate). The respondent receives personal service of a summons with some information about the place and time of the hearing and his rights to counsel. Under current practice in various states, he may or may not receive specific information about the allegations against him. Substantial pressure exists, however, for full and informative disclosure to the respondent of all the allegations against him, presented by a court employee in plain clothes, who spends time with the respondent explaining his rights (*Lessard vs. Schmidt*, 1972; *Recommended Judicial Practices*; ABA, 1989). After functional assessment is ordered and carried out, the judge considers that evidence and other data put before a hearing and selects the remedy appropriate for the respondent's situation.

It is at this time that the form of the functional evaluation report becomes important. While judges are overwhelmed by reading material, much of it is intensely dull. A report consisting of checklists or scores on standardized tests is likely to be skimmed and considered only momentarily. A concise but vivid narrative report, however, can draw a realistic picture of the respondent that no court can ignore. If it is accompanied by more standard data, fine—but an evaluator should not lose the opportunity to present an accurate and living portrait. Where the judge chooses a remedy other that the one petitioned for, he has several alternatives available. He can dismiss the inappropriate petition and order refiling for the proper remedy. He can render the appropriate judgment and file the order, instructing counsel to amend the pleadings to conform with the result. If the functional evaluation convinces the judge that the requested remedy is inappropriate, he can set up a pretrial conference, instruct both sides on the probable outcome, and invite amended filings.

Some authorities have recommended alternate dispute resolution approaches such as mediation in these situations. If alternate dispute resolution is chosen, the facts are considered by an appointed, nonjudicial mediator, and recommendations for action are made to the parties. It is hoped that mediation can succeed in reducing institutionalization and overprotection while assuring the at-risk respondent of a network of assistance in the community (*Judicial Practices*, ABA, 1989).

Another method for getting from the requested remedy to a more appropriate one would require a sort of unified protective statute, where procedures for all three remedies could be specified, and the fact finder would apply the one statute to each individual case. It is easy to recommend legislative change in an article like this, and very difficult to achieve the desired result in the real and political world. This suggestion, therefore, is included only to round out the discussion.

Potential Problems in Using the Judicial Menu Notice

Because of the potential for limitation of personal freedom, proper notice to the respondent of the nature of the proceedings has been held to be jurisdictional for mental illness commitment and guardianship (Parry, 1985). Extension of this requirement to involuntary imposition of adult protective services is included in state APS statutes. If the court is free to change the nature of the proceedings upon receipt of functional evaluation data, how can sufficient notice be assured? This is a particular problem where the respondent is not required to appear, but should be a concern in any case; the respondent's counsel who is prepared to defend a guardianship may not be ready to defend a mental illness commitment. While some delay is inevitable, the nature of these cases argues for speedy resolution.

A fair and appropriate notice could include information that the court will consider best interests of the respondent and the options available to him, resources available in the community, and institutionalization only where no less restrictive alternative is available. It would also inform the respondent that an investigator would be visiting him in the near future, to gather information for the court about his abilities to care for himself safely. To give proper notice, the summons would also have to state that the court would consider his mental health, and inform the respondent of the possibility of involuntary imposition of services. Managing so threatening a notice in a humane, comprehensible, and informative way presents a very real challenge!

Judicial Insecurity with Diagnostic/ Therapeutic Role

Few judges are comfortable with the responsibility for assessing and predicting human behavior, although in fact they do it every day. They are taught to decide the question presented, not to invent new and broader questions, nor to expand the scope of inquiry. (Many have, however, particularly on questions of great social importance.) As we noted initially, the menu approach invites consideration of a different, broader question—a question which, nonetheless, remains within the equitable jurisdiction of probate courts. We suspect that many judges use the menu as a matter of course, but have not formalized it as a theoretical model.

Evaluators who are court employees can help judges to become more at ease with what is, really, an insoluble problem. Professionals in all fields grapple with predicting the future. Judges are just as uncomfortable with these decisions as physicians, therapists, and social scientists. At best, it is an educated guess.

Overprotection

Finally, there is real concern for the potentially repressive nature of a "plenary" protective view (Frolik, 1981). Where judges feel free to use the full range of these remedies, there is a substantial risk of overprotection. Petitioners, attorneys, and judges in these troublesome cases naturally seek a permanent solution to the problems; no one relishes having to oversee and revise a care plan indefinitely. This is the basis for resistance to limited guardianships, periodic rehearings for the chronically mentally ill, and community-based care for those in need of adult protective services. The pressure on probate courts to clear the docket mitigates against ongoing court supervision of incapacitated elders. Those who advocate what Folik calls the "therapeutic state" must perpetually advocate for the greatest possible civil liberty within it, since society's normal desire to have the situation settled—with the kindest possible motives—poses a real threat to clients.

Despite the danger of misuse which exists with any technique or innovation, the use of a judicial menu in dealing with the incapacitated elderly who have been functionally evaluated has real potential for improving the appropriateness of remedies in our probate courts.

REFERENCES

American Bar Association (1979). *Model Guardianship Statute*, sec. 3(2), (4).

American Bar Association Commission on Legal Problems of the Elderly (1986). *Statement of recommended judicial practices adopted by the national conference of the judiciary on guardianship proceedings for the elderly*. Washington, D.C.: ABA.

American Bar Association Commission on the Mentally Disabled and Commission on Legal Problems of the Elderly (1989). *Guardianship: An agenda for reform*. Washington, D.C.: ABA.

Beis, E., (1983). State Involuntary Commitment Statutes. *Mental Disability Law Reporter*, 7, 358-369.

Frolik, L.A., (1981). Plenary guardianship: An analysis, a critique, and a proposal for reform. *Arizona Law Review 23*, 599-660.

In re Boyer, 636 P. 2d 1085 (Utah 1981).

Johnson, J.C. & Mezy, M.D. (1989). Functional status assessment: An approach to tertiary prevention. In R. Lavizzo-Mourey, S.C.

Day, D. Diserens & J.A. Grisso, (Eds.), *Practicing prevention for the elderly* (pp. 141-152). Philadelphia: Hanley & Belfus.

Lawton, M.P. (1971). The functional assessment of elderly people. *Journal of the American Gerontological Society*, *19*, 465-481.

Lessard v. Schmidt, 349 F. Supp. 1078 (E.D. Wis. 1972).

Matter of Adult Protective Services for Hartman, 518 N.E. 2d 482 (Ind. App. 1987).

N.H. Rev. Stat. Ann. Sec. 464-A (1983).

Nolan, B.S. (1984). Functional evaluation of the elderly in guardianship proceedings. *Law, Medicine & Health Care*, *12*, 210-218.

Ohio Rev. Code Annot. sec. 5101.60 (1981).

Parry, J. (1985). Incompetence, guardianship, and restoration. In S. Brakel, J. Parry, B. & Weiner (Eds). *The mentally disabled and the law*, (p. 380). Chicago, IL: American Bar Foundation.

Saunders, A.G., Jr. & Simon, M.M. (1987). Individual functional assessment: An instruction manual. *Mental & Physical Disability Law Reporter*, *11*, 60-70.

Van Duizend, R., McGraw, B.D., & Keilitz, I. (1984). An overview of state involuntary civil commitment statutes. *Mental & Physical Disability Law Reporter*, *8*, 328.

Material Abuse of the Elderly: When Is Guardianship a Solution?

Kathleen H. Wilber, PhD

SUMMARY. During the last decade, the area of elder abuse has received increasing attention from researchers, providers, advocates, and policy makers. Although studies on elder abuse indicate that misappropriation of assets is not uncommon, material abuse represents an area that has not been addressed. Using a case study approach, this article analyzes two material abuse situations. Issues raised in the case studies are used to develop criteria for appraising potential material abuse situations and offering guidelines for assessing the appropriateness of guardianship as a means of protecting victims of material abuse.

There have been frequent debates on the prevalence of elder abuse and numerous discussions about what constitutes abuse, yet no consensus has emerged (Galbraith, 1989; Hudson, 1986; Sprey & Matthews, 1989; Vaughan & Ingman, 1989). In an area known for its muddy waters, one of the murkiest definitional areas is that of financial exploitation or material abuse. Although elder abuse has emerged as a major area of research and policy development over the last decade, material abuse has received little attention. Perhaps this gap is best explained by the major paradigm used to

Kathleen H. Wilber is Assistant Professor of Gerontology at the University of Southern California. Address correspondence to the author at the Andrus Gerontology Center, MC 0191, University of Southern California, Los Angeles, CA 90089-0191.

This research was supported in part by Grant No. 90AM0153 from the Office of Human Development and The Center for the Public Interest. The support of both organizations is gratefully acknowledged. The author thanks Leah Buturain, Nahed Guirguis, and Karen Harter.

conceptualize elder abuse, that of domestic violence. Sprey and Matthews, (1989) have suggested that this orientation limits the scope of research on elder mistreatment to the area of physical and emotional abuse.

The prevalence of material abuse is not known, but several studies indicate that it is a significant problem. Data of substantiated elder abuse from a study in Illinois found that material abuse occurred in 53% of the cases and represented the most frequent type of abuse reported (Hwalek, Hill & Stahl, 1989). Wolf, Godkin and Pillemer (1984) found material abuse in 35.9% of the cases they studied and indicated that victims of material abuse were more apt to be single than victims of other types of abuse. Schmidt et al. (1981) noted that frail elderly victims of material abuse comprise "at least one-third of the caseloads of some public guardians" (p.175). Steinberg's study of the Los Angeles Office of the Public Guardian (1985) revealed that approximately one-third of all referrals resulted from the need to protect assets.

WHAT IS MATERIAL ABUSE?

A number of terms are used to describe misuse of an elder's assets. Material abuse is referred to as financial exploitation, exploitation of resources, material exploitation, fiduciary abuse, financial mistreatment, financial maltreatment, financial victimization, economic victimization, extortion, theft, and fraud. Elder abuse statutes in several states refer to the need to protect elders from "designing persons," "improvidence," and "swindlers." The term material abuse is used throughout this paper as a generic term which includes misappropriation of property, possession, and financial assets.

As with much of the elder abuse literature, a standard definition of what constitutes material abuse has proved to be elusive. This lack of clarity creates practical problems for elders and their advocates because an allegation of material abuse, however it is defined, may result in guardianship proceedings (Schmidt et al., 1981). While guardianship may be appropriate in a number of such cases, it represents a highly restrictive intervention that should only be initiated under well-defined conditions and when less restrictive approaches have been ruled out.

Several factors appear to contribute to the perspective that referral for guardianship is an appropriate redress in cases of material abuse. These include (1) age-based reporting requirements for elder abuse, (2) the lack of viable service alternatives, (3) interpersonal dynamics of co-dependency and loyalty which may inhibit the elder's recognition of the problem and willingness to deal with the abuse, and (4) conceptual confusion about the relationship of material abuse to other forms of abuse and neglect.

Current elder abuse policies focus primarily on reporting requirements rather than treatment. Almost one-third of the states' elder abuse statutes use age as the sole criterion for reporting (Thobaben, 1989), rather than applying criteria related to dependency and functional status, thus ignoring the capacity of the elder to make decisions (Crystal, 1987). For example, California's elder abuse reporting law (AB 3988) states that "'fiduciary abuse' means a situation in which any person who has the care or custody of, or who stands in a position of trust to an elder or a dependent adult, takes, secretes, or appropriates their money or property, to any use or purpose not in the due and lawful execution of his or her trust"[1] (Section 4.f). A brochure summarizes this definition as: "The mismanagement of money or stealing of property belonging to an elderly person" (Los Angeles County Elder Abuse Hotline, 1988). Similarly, the definition of material abuse used in Illinois is: "The use of an elderly person's resources to the disadvantage of the elder or for the profit/advantage of a person other than the elder" (Hwalek, Hill & Stahl, 1989, p. 198). Such age-based reporting requirements criminalize relationships and behavior that would not be considered problematic for younger adults. They also result in confusion about when intervention should occur and what sort of help is required (Callahan, 1988).

This confusion is exacerbated by the lack of viable service alternatives. Steinberg's study (1985) indicated that persons turn to guardianship when they feel they have exhausted other alternatives. Yet the Los Angeles County Office of the Public Guardian ruled that 80% of those referred were inappropriate for guardianship. While the gap between existing services and guardianship could be narrowed by services such as money management, public and private commitment to develop such services has been limited (Buturain, 1987).

Spray and Matthews (1989) suggested the need to expand elder abuse concepts from a focus on the individual "victim" to the area of relationship and reciprocity between those involved in the abusive situation. Findings presented in this article support this expanded focus and illustrate that interpersonal dynamics between the elder and the perpetrator, and issues such as loyalty and co-dependency are important dynamics of material abuse. The elder's relationship with the perpetrator, often a family member or significant other, may inhibit the elder from addressing the situation in a socially desirable way.

Finally, material abuse often occurs in conjunction with other forms of abuse. Although it has been suggested that different forms of abuse have different etiologies (Cicirelli, 1986), the presence of material abuse in combination with other forms is striking. An analysis of the Administration on Aging's Model Projects On Elderly Abuse found that the majority (73%) of elder abuse cases involved more than one type of victimization (Wolf, 1986; Wolf, Godkin & Pillemer, 1984). Segal and Iris (1989) also noted a majority of cases (59%) involving multiple abuse. Another Administration on Aging funded program, The Guardianship Diversion Program (GDP), upon which this article is based, found that in over two-thirds of the cases, suspected or known material abuse was accompanied by neglect. In some instances, a neglected, socially isolated elder, most often suffering from cognitive impairment, appeared to represent an easy mark for material abuse. In other instances the older person was placed in the double jeopardy of abuse and neglect by an unscrupulous relative or caretaker who exhausted resources needed for the care of the older persons. A third confound occurred when a family member or provider attempted to intervene on behalf of a resistant elder only to be confronted with the double bind of neglecting the individual or forcing an intervention that was unacceptable to the elder.

Guardianship and Material Abuse

Schmidt et al., (1981) has suggested that we examine ". . . the need for guardianship in order to prevent the victimization of the frail elderly" (p.175). When material abuse is suspected, appointment to guardianship may be seen as the only option. Guardianship may be viewed as an acceptable solution because such surrogate decision-making insures that someone has been legally appointed to represent the interests of the ward. It also provides for legal remedies if property and assets are not managed appropriately. Ostensibly, guardianship involves a modicum of monitoring, record keeping, and judicial oversight, although in practice, this oversight may be minimal or non-existent.

METHODS

The Guardianship Diversion Project (GDP) was conducted to evaluate the effectiveness of money management as an alternative to guardianship and to learn about characteristics of persons referred for guardianship. Subjects (n = 63) were persons 60 years of age or older who were referred to the Los Angeles County Office of Public Guardian or Los Angeles County Adult Protective Services because of concern over their inability to manage money and/or assets. Most were considered to be at risk of guardianship because of abuse, neglect, and/or extreme frailty.

Subjects participated in a semi-structured interview in their homes every 6 months for a period of 12 to 24 months. Interviewers gathered basic demographic information as well as measures of cognitive functioning, depression, activity limitations (ADLS and IADS), social supports, service utilization, psychiatric symptoms, and financial hardship. Six rational scales from the CORE-CARE and SHORT-CARE (Comprehensive Assessment and Referral Evaluation) instruments and one global rating scale were used (Gurland, 1977).

Characteristics of the Subjects

Subjects evidenced high levels of cognitive impairment, activity limitations, social isolation, and depression. (Findings are reported in Wilber, 1988.) Over 40% (n = 27) of the cases involved confirmed or suspected material abuse. In the majority of the cases, perpetrators were known to the victim: forty-four percent were family members; less than one-fifth were strangers. Persons who were known or suspected of being victimized were differentiated from those where material abuse was not in evidence in only one area, self-reported financial limitations ($r = .58$, $P < .001$).

CASE EXAMPLES

Cases in which material abuse was present often posed problems for those attempting to initiate an intervention. These cases illustrate a number of complex issues endemic to the study of adult exploitation and the ethical dilemmas inherent in choosing between competing values. Victims were often reluctant to permit intervention or to initiate changes in their relationship with their exploiters. As a result, most were resistant to becoming involved with social service providers. Thus, the provider was often left with the conflict of ignoring the problem or initiating guardianship against the expressed will of the elder.

Case Example One, Mr. D.

Mr. D., an 82-year-old widower, was referred by the local police department following allegations that several men, who resided with him, were financially exploiting him. He was subsequently referred to the GDP. When the interviewers arrived, they found three men living in his small two-bedroom home, one of whom shared a bed with Mr. D. The "boarders" were all known to have criminal records. At the request of one of the men, Mr. D. had taken a second mortgage on his home. Over time he had given away the cash. As the monthly loan payment was in excess of his income, Mr. D. had no way to repay the debt. Mr. D. had made frequent "loans" to all of the men. None had been repaid.

Apparently one or more of the men had lived with Mr. D. for the three preceding years. During that time several other men had moved into the house, some taking up residence on a permanent basis while others stayed for only short periods of time. In addition to the mortgage money, during the three year period in which the "boarders" lived with him, Mr. D. had almost completely exhausted his savings of $30,000. Case records and verbal reports from the caseworkers suggested that Mr. D. was "passive, compliant, eager to please, and highly impressionable." While he appeared to be lonely and socially isolated, one worker suggested that he lacked the intelligence to take care of himself and described him as "naive, not very bright, and unable to look out for his best interests."

When the interviewers called on Mr. D., he appeared robust, alert, and eager to participate. He readily agreed to take part in the study indicating that he was happy to do whatever the researchers asked of him. Mr. D. correctly answered all questions on the Cognitive Impairment Scale; denied experiencing any sadness, regret, or unhappiness, and indicated that he was self-sufficient with ADLs and IADLs. Problems identified during a one hour assessment included anxiety about money, financial hardship, and social isolation.

Mr. D.'s wife had managed the family finances until her death several years before the boarders arrived. He had not heard from his only relative, a brother, who lived in New York, for over thirty years. Mr. D. divulged that he had always been for the underdog, enjoyed giving money to his friends, and would do it again if he had the money. He also acknowledged that he was receiving sexual favors, validation, and a modicum of companionship in exchange for money, room, and board. However costly these companions proved to be, Mr. D. appeared to be willing, for a time, to pay the price. However, once the consequences became clear (foreclosure on his home) he grew increasingly ambivalent about continuing the relationships. He began to complain that his friends were noisy and indicated that he was concerned that they were taking drugs. He also expressed distress that they were not repaying him and reported that he had given them some of the money to pay his bills for him.

Initially, Mr. D. had refused help from the social service agency that had been referred to assist him. But, when it became clear that he would lose his home because he was unable to make his mortgage payments he sought their help. A durable power of attorney was arranged. And, with Mr. D.'s knowledge and consent, his home was sold, his debts were paid and he was placed in a Board and Care. Soon his former friends began to visit and request loans eroding the small savings recouped from the sale of his home. Mr. D., faced with a shrinking bank account, grew disenchanted with the social service agency and began to blame them for the loss of his home. He cancelled the power of attorney. Shortly after, he received a modest inheritance from his brother and it appeared that this, too, would be spent on "loans."[2]

Case Example Two, Mrs. E.

Mrs. E., 92, lived alone with her 12 cats in a large home filled with antiques. She was described by the referral source as "not able to properly take care of her affairs . . . and not able to provide a clear picture of her resources" which, from all accounts were considerable. Although physical frailty was mentioned in the initial referral, the interviewer described Mrs. E. as "agile" and noted that she "walked fast and jumped up and down to show the interviewer things." Mrs. E., by her own account, could not manage her property. She had, therefore, employed someone whom she trusted, her gardener, Mr. A., to handle her financial affairs. Although she was apparently willing to give him considerable sums of money (she thought she had told him he could have $25,000 to buy a home), he withdrew in excess of $40,000 for his personal use. Mr. A. "earned" this money by serving as the gardener, handyman, errand-man, shopping assistant, chauffeur and bookkeeper. Case records describe Mrs. E. as "dressed in ragged clothes which were torn and stained. Her shoes were full of holes . . . chairs were covered with rags . . . a disconnected refrigerator contained rotting food . . . tables covered with newspaper, house dirty, all locks on the doors appear to be broken." According to a neighbor, Mr. A. had broken the locks every time the neighbor had replaced them. Mrs. E., concerned about the locks, stated that she "sleeps on the couch to look for burglars." Mr. A. assisted Mrs. E. with the weekly shopping, and used her money to purchase food for himself as well. Mr. A.'s family has borrowed money from Mrs. E. And, Mr. A. had moved people into the home during a three month period when Mrs. E. was in a nursing home. Mrs. E. told the interviewer that she turned over her affairs to Mr. A. because she trusted him but admitted, "he never gave me anything he just takes."

Although she described herself as fairly happy, in response to interview questions, she answered that she had enjoyed almost nothing during the past month, felt lonely and wished she were dead. Mrs. E. missed four out of the eleven questions used to assess cognitive functioning, was unable to describe her financial situation to the interviewer, and evidenced little ability to see that her basic needs were met. During the interview, she admitted that she worried about money and hoped Mr. A. would not take any more. Mrs. E. had told her neighbor that Mr. A. had "raped her and had sex with her." Mr. A. had persuaded Mrs. E. to change her will leaving most of her property to him.

DISCUSSION

There are several similarities between these cases. Both illustrate the complexity of material abuse, the reciprocal relationship between "perpetrator" and "victim," and the problem of providing effective treatment that satisfies the personal preferences of the elder. Both cases elicit feelings of sympathy and anger. The motives of the perpetrator appear to be exclusively self-serving; the assets lost are considerable. The elderly "victim" is isolated and lonely and the perpetrator represents the most significant relationship available to the older person. The implicit contract for both individuals is that they would like outside help to protect their assets but they are unwilling to jeopardize their relationships. A sexual relationship with the perpetrator is a factor in both cases. Although the nature of the relationship is less clear in Mrs. E.'s case and may involve sexual abuse, neither Mr. D. nor Mrs. E. wishes to terminate their relationship.

Both Mr. D. and Mrs. E. indicated that they were not interested in changing their current relationships. Both confirmed that they had given extensive amounts of money in exchange for valued services. Both acknowledged that they consented to doing so and were willing to continue doing so, although they expressed anxiety about the arrangement. Both had suffered dire consequences as a result of their agreements. While Mrs. E. had adequate assets, they were not being used in her interests. Mr. D. had lost most of his assets including his home. It was probable that he would lose his remaining assets. Without intervention in the form of guardianship, there was concern that he would end up on the street. But, Mr. D. appeared more willing to accept that outcome than he was to accept assistance.

In analyzing the cases, several factors need to be considered. First, are either Mr. D. or Mrs. C. victims of material abuse? Second, does guardianship offer an appropriate solution?

Assessing Material Abuse

The most straightforward method of identifying material abuse is the degree to which fraud, theft or coercion is used to obtain assets. If one or more is present, the situation may be defined as material abuse. Fraud implies that deception, or theft through misrepresentation, is occurring. Several cases from the GDP involved instances where older persons were lead to believe that their money was being used for a specified purpose only to learn that it was being spent by the perpetrator. Several others were providing monetary support in exchange for a guarantee that they would not be institutionalized; a guarantee that was not always honored. Although this article does not deal with the area of consumer fraud, it should be noted here that consumer fraud appears to be an increasing problem. Victims are often isolated and/or suffering from cognitive impairment. While such fraud may be the most insidious form of material abuse, it is rarely addressed (McGhee, 1983).

In contrast to deception, some of the GDP cases of material abuse involved direct theft, or appropriation of money or assets without the knowledge or consent of the elder. And at least one involved coercion, forcing the elder to provide money or assets through threats or intimidation. Applying these definitions, it appears that Mrs. E.'s, is a victim of theft and possibly of coercion; clearly she is a victim of neglect and quite possibly a victim of abuse as well. However, her case illustrates the difficulty of determining what has transpired when the victim suffers from cognitive impairment. It is clear that she gave Mr. A. permission to take money and valuables. It is not clear how much money and under what terms.

Mr. D., in contrast does not appear to be a victim of material abuse. Although he had complained, on at least one occasion, that he had provided money to his friends to pay bills for him and they had not done so, he seemed uninterested in pursuing the matter, and, in fact, continued to provide money whenever it was requested. It appears that there was neither deceit nor coercion and there is no evidence of direct theft.

Decision to Initiate Guardianship

The decision to initiate guardianship should be based on a careful assessment of the elder's cognitive capacity to understand his/her situation and its ramifications. Cognitive impairment that inhibits an elder's ability to manage his/her affairs in combination with suspected material abuse requires substitute judgement. In such cases, a court appointed guardian may be the best solution if judicial oversight is performed. Less restrictive alternatives, such as money management, may be effective in some situations, but such services are not available in many places. Furthermore, they are often ineffective with resistant clients (Wilber, 1988). Many do not include safeguards of monitoring and oversight. And finally, with the exception of durable power of attorney and representative payee, most alternatives do not carry the authority to make decisions for persons with moderate to severe levels of cognitive impairment.

Mrs. E. does not appear capable of ensuring that her basic needs are met and evidences little insight into her financial situation or the ramifications of placing Mr. A. in charge of her affairs. Thus, initiating guardianship is warranted assuming reversible causes of cognitive impairment have been ruled out.

In contrast, Mr. D., while also evidencing poor judgement, displays no signs of cognitive impairment. If poor judgement, in the absence of cognitive impairment, does not constitute a significant reason to impose guardianship, are there other criteria that support a decision in favor of guardianship? Although cognitive capacity represents the appropriate criterion for determining guardianship, current policies and practices may encourage the use of other factors such as age, protection of the victim's assets, and the social desirability of the elder's decisions and their outcomes.

As discussed earlier, age, in some states serves as a surrogate for incapacity or incompetence (Crystal, 1987). In assessing the need for protective intervention, it is important to "take age out of the equation." Support Services for Seniors, a money management program in San Francisco, does this by asking providers to assume another age for the client and to consider, for example, how they would approach the case if the "victim" were in his thirties or forties (McKay, 1987). Since Mr. D. does not evidence incapacity then it is inappropriate to initiate guardianship solely because he is in his ninth decade.

Apart from the issue of capacity, protection of assets could be construed as a rationale for guardianship intervention. Although Mr. D. made decisions which jeopardized his assets, he had decided that providing money to his "friends" was what he wanted to do. In an interview with the author two years after he lost his home, Mr. D. said that he would do the same thing again if given the opportunity. And, if he had access to money at that time he would give it away. Only with Mr. D.'s consent should efforts be made to protect his assets.

Protection of assets does not provide a rationale for imposing guardianship against an elder's will. Similarly, guardianship should not be used for "social control," to impose decisions on elders that meet with the agenda of their families, neighbors or friends (Quinn & Tomita, 1986). Although Mr. D.'s decisions to support persons who were considered undesirable, unsavory and abusive by his family, his neighbors, service providers and the police jeopardized his financial well being and to some extent his safety, guardianship is inappropriate. While it may well have been painful for Mr. D.'s family to witness what they considered offensive behavior on his part and despicable behavior on the part of his "associates," it is neither the family's nor the provider's role to control Mr. D.'s behavior. Nor is it appropriate for the neighbors, even with their legitimate concern about the impact Mr. D.'s behavior was having on the neighborhood, to seek guardianship as a means of dealing with the problem. Other legal remedies could have been initiated against

Mr. D. which would force him to assume responsibility for his home (i.e., noise complaints, too many unrelated persons in an area zoned for single family homes, etc.).

CONCLUSION

Material abuse represents a complex unexplored problem area, fraught with difficult service delivery issues and ethical dilemmas. Two similar cases have been presented in an effort to develop and apply criteria for assessing the appropriateness of guardianship as an intervention in cases of material abuse. It has been argued that Mr. D. has the cognitive capacity to understand the consequences of his actions, thus it is inappropriate to initiate guardianship against his will. In contrast, Mrs. E.'s inability to evaluate, understand, and manage her situation, coupled with material abuse, suggests that, in her case, guardianship is needed.

Guardianship may represent a welcome solution to families and providers who have exhausted less restrictive alternatives. Certainly for Mrs. E. it is the solution that best addresses the problem. This does not mean, however, that it is always the best solution. The question should always be asked, whose interest is guardianship serving? Mrs. E.'s placement under guardianship was less costly to her than her previous arrangement. The neighbor's needs for security were enhanced and the Department of Social Services was able to close the case. Mrs. E.'s needs for safety, housing and adequate health care were satisfied. Because guardianship is an effective way to address multiple needs, however, should not persuade us that it is the right solution. It represents a response of last resort which should not be entered into unless the criterion of capacity has been met and less restrictive alternatives are ruled out.

Similarly, deciding against guardianship for Mr. D., leaves many questions unanswered. While the solution for Mrs. E. is quite circumscribed, Mr. D.'s situation continues to be messy and uncomfortable for those involved. Mr. D. is likely to continue to spend down his savings until ultimately he becomes eligible for public benefits. Thus, this "solution" is likely to increase public costs. Costs also may be incurred by continued involvement or reinvolvement of service providers who pursue the range of possible means for assisting Mr. D. While guardianship for Mr. D. is not recommended, neither is retreating from the case altogether. The most effective approach is to continue to provide ongoing support to Mr. D. combined with assurance that help is available if he should decide that he needs it. Although the multiple needs of clients in the GDP often required assistance of this magnitude, many social service providers do not have the resources to provide such ongoing monitoring.

The resolution of Mrs. E.'s material abuse gives us a sense of effectiveness, while cases like Mr. D. offer the greatest challenge. Such cases require adherence to the value of client choice and the standard of less restrictive, appropriate alternative. Persistent support and monitoring is required, but results are often disappointing. Such cases should serve to remind us that the role of the service provider is not to solve the client's problem, but to support the client's efforts to solve his own problems while respecting his right to live according to his own values and wishes.[3]

NOTES

1. "'elder' means any person residing in this state, 65 years of age or older."

2. This case illustrates the problem of the effectiveness of the money management program and durable power of attorney over time. In a state of acute crisis, Mr. D. permitted, even sought, assistance. Once the crisis had abated he was reluctant to continue receiving services. If the person is not "incompetent" a durable power of attorney is revokable at any time. The case also raises ethical considerations about when and what types of intervention are appropriate.

3. This course of action was pursued with Mr.D. Ultimately he requested help and guardianship proceedings were initiated with his consent. He expressed relief that he would not lose his remaining assests. Although he remains estranged from his family, he is visited occasionally by his former boarders. Two months after Mrs. E. was interviewed, a private conservator was appointed by the Court to handle her financial affairs, and she was placed in a nursing home.

REFERENCES

Buturain, L. (1987). *National survey of daily money management programs*, unpublished. Andrus Gerontology Center.

Callahan, J.J. (1988). Elder abuse: Some questions for policymakers. *The Gerontologist*, Vol. 28, No. 4, 453-458.

California Legislation Assembly. (1986). AB 3988, chapter 769. *Elder dependent adult abuse*, Sacramento.

Cicirelli, V.G. (1986). The helping relationship and family neglect in later life. In K.A. Pillemer & R.S. Wolf (Eds.), *Elder abuse: Conflict in the family* (pp. 49-66) Massachusetts: Auburn House Publishing Company.

Crystal, S. (1987). Elder abuse: The latest "crisis." *The Public Interest*, 88, 56-66.

Galbraith, Michael W. (1989). A critical examination of the definitional, methodological, and theoretical problems of elder abuse. In R. Filinson & S.R. Ingman (Eds.), *Elder Abuse: Practice and policy* (pp. 35-42) New York: Human Sciences Press, Inc.

Gurland, B.J., Kuriansky, J., Sharpe, L., Simon, R., Stiller, P. and Birkett, P. (1977). The comprehensive assessment and referral evaluation (CARE): Rational, development and reliability, *International Journal of Aging and Human Development*, 8:9-42.

Hudson, M. F. (1986). Elder Mistreatment: Current research. In K.A. Pillemer and R. S. Wolf (Eds.), *Elder abuse: Conflict in the family* (pp. 125-149) Massachusetts: Auburn House Publishing Company.

Hwalek, M., Hill, B. and Stahl, C. (1989). The Illinois plan for a state wide elder abuse program. In R. Filinson & S.R. Ingman (Eds.), *Elder abuse: Practice and policy* (pp. 196-207) New York: Human Sciences Press, Inc.

Los Angeles County Elder Abuse Hotline (1988). A joint brochure publicizing *Elder Abuse Hotline* by Public Social Services, Community and Senior Citizens Services, Health Services, and Mental Health.

McGee, J.L. (1983). The vulnerability of elderly consumers. *International Journal of Aging and Human Development*, 17 (3).

McKay, J. (1987). Personal Communication.

Quinn, M.J., & Tomita, S.K. (1986). *Elder abuse and neglect – Causes, diagnosis, and intervention strategies*. New York: Springer.

Regan, J.J. (1983). Protective services for the elderly: Benefit or threat. In J.I. Kosberg (Ed.), *Abuse and maltreatment of the elderly: Causes and interventions* (pp. 279-291) Massachusetts: John Wright. PSG, Inc.

Schmidt, W.C., Miller, K.S., Bell, W.G., New, B.E. (1981). *Public guardianship and the elderly*. Cambridge, Massachusetts: Ballinger Publishing Company.

Segal, S.R. & Iris, M.A. (1989). The use of legal interventions in a systems approach to casework. In R. Filinson & S.R. Ingman (Eds.), *Elder abuse: Practice and policy* (pp. 104-116) New York: Human Sciences Press, Inc.

Sprey, J. and Matthews, S.H. (1989). The perils of drawing policy implications from research: The case of elder mistreatment. In R. Filinson & S.R. Ingman (Eds.), *Elder abuse: Practice and Policy* (pp. 51-61) New York: Human Sciences Press, Inc.

Steinberg, R.M. (1985). *Alternative approaches to conservatorship and protection of older adults referred to public guardian*. Andrus Gerontology Center.

Trobaben, M. (1989). State elder/adult abuse and protective laws. In R. Filinson

& S.R. Ingman (Eds.), *Elder abuse: Practice and policy* (pp. 138-152) New York: Human Sciences Press, Inc.

Vaughan, S.E., Ingman, S.R. (1989). Reconceptualizing elder abuse. *Gerontology Review*, Volume 2, (1), 77-84.

Wilber, K.H. (1988). *Evaluation of guardianship/conservatorship and institutionalization diversion national demonstration project.* Andrus Gerontology Center.

Wolf, R.S. (1986). Major findings from three model projects on elderly abuse. In K.A. Pillemer & R.S. Wolf (Eds.), *Elder abuse: Conflict in the family* (pp. 218-238) Massachusetts: Auburn Publishing Company.

Wolf, R.S., Godkin, M.K., and Pillemer, K.A. (1984). *Elder abuse and neglect: Final Report from three model projects and Appendixes 1 and 2*. Worcester; University of Massachusetts, Medical Center and University Center on Aging. (ERIC Document Reproduction on Service No. Ed 254796).

Elderly Nursing Home Residents' Need for Public Guardianship Services in Tennessee

David Hightower, BSN
Alex Heckert, MA
Winsor Schmidt, JD, LLM

SUMMARY. This study assesses the need for public limited guardian, conservator, representative payee, and power of attorney services among elderly nursing home residents in Tennessee in the Summer and Fall of 1988. Of the 295 licensed nursing homes in Tennessee, 123 responded that 32% of their residents were receiving one of the services, and 10% of their residents (1,044 of 10,555) needed one of the services. As many as 3,003 residents in Tennessee may need one of the services. The effects of size and location of nursing homes are measurable but minimal. The problems of record-keeping and conflict of interest are cited.

BACKGROUND

In July 1986, the Tennessee legislature established a program of public guardianship for the elderly to be administered by the Tennessee Commission on Aging. Section 34-7-101 of the Tennessee

David Hightower is a nurse at the Memphis Veterans Administration Hospital and an MPA candidate in the Department of Political Science at Memphis State University in Memphis, TN 38152. Alex Heckert is Visiting Assistant Professor and PhD Candidate in the Department of Political Science at Memphis State University in Memphis, TN 38152. Winsor Schmidt is Associate Professor at Pace University School of Law, 78 North Broadway, White Plains, NY 10603.

The financial support of the Memphis State University Public Service Program and the cooperation of the nursing home survey respondents are very much appreciated.

Code Annotated (TCA), entitled "Public Guardianship for the Elderly Law," was created with the intent to establish a statewide program of public guardianship for those disabled persons sixty (60) years of age or older. The program was designed for those who are unable to meet the essential requirements for their physical health or to manage essential aspects of their financial resources. Many elderly have no willing and responsible family member or friend to serve as guardian, or resources to compensate a private guardian. For those who qualify as indigent under SSI guidelines, the state imposes no fees or costs of any kind against the ward's estate.

Recent data obtained from the Tennessee Commission on Aging public guardianship program show that 215 total clients were served by the program during the quarter of October-December 1988 (Schmidt & Heckert, 1989). Of these 215, 117 clients required full guardianship: 98 required alternatives services: limited guardianship (18), representative payee/legal custodian (54), guardian ad litem (13), and power of attorney (13). Potential wards are referred to the public guardian program district agencies from various sources, including family members, nursing home staff, hospital staff, adult protection services, attorneys, and other interested persons.

For a state the size of Tennessee, with a population of approximately 517,588 individuals over the age of 65 in 1980, it seems likely that some dysfunctional, socially isolated elderly are falling through the gaps in the system. The purpose of this study is to assess the extent of need for public guardianship among elderly nursing home residents in Tennessee. Is there substantial unmet need for public guardianship among elderly nursing home residents in Tennessee? No such assessment has been made to date by the state or by the Commission on Aging which administers the program.

DEFINITIONS

As used in this study, the term "ward" is defined from the Tennessee statute as a disable person sixty (60) years of age or older who has been placed under the protection of a public guardian by the court due to the person's inability to meet the essential requirements for personal physical health, or to manage the essential aspects of personal financial resources, and who has no willing and responsible family member or friend to serve as a guardian, or resources to compensate a private guardian. A "disabled person" means any person determined by the court to be in need of partial or full supervision, protection and assistance by reason of mental illness, physical illness or injury, advanced age, developmental disability or other mental or physical incapacity. "Public guardian" in Tennessee is defined as an employee of the state appointed by the court to serve as limited guardian, guardian ad litem, or conservator, or authorized by statute to serve as representative payee or to accept power of attorney. "Limited guardian" means any person appointed by the court to manage, supervise or protect a disabled person, to the extent ordered by the court. A "guardian ad litem" is any person appointed by the court to represent the ward during court proceedings. It is not necessary that the guardian ad litem be an attorney. A "conservator" is anyone appointed by the court to have charge and management of the property of a disabled person, and if the court deems it advisable, also to have custody of the person subject to the direction of the court. It should be noted that in the language of the conservatorship statute, section 34-4-202 of the TCA, ". . . no person will be penalized for choosing to proceed under one law [conservatorship] as opposed to the other [limited guardianship]." The Tennessee legislature specifically intended the Conservatorship Law of 1980 as an alternative method to the limited guardianship law that deals with estates of incompetents and disabled persons.

REVIEW OF LITERATURE

Guardianship is a concept that has been recognized since the time of Cicero and Plutarch. Current perspectives have evolved from English common law. The responsibility for administering the property of a person judged to be "incompetent" is entrusted to a relative or willing friend until such time as the disabled person recovers. Guardianship is based upon the doctrine of "parens patriae" (literally, "father of his country") which attributes to the state (or sovereign) both the right, and the duty, to protect the persons and property of those unable to care for themselves. Guardianship confers upon one individual the right and authority to make decisions regarding the management of another person's estate, material possessions, or personal affairs (Alexander, 1975,1977; Langen, 1978: Schmidt, 1985).

As a protective intervention, guardianship is receiving increasing attention as a strategy for protecting persons at risk from exploitation, abuse, and neglect. However, since the autonomy of the ward is so greatly affected, often resulting in the deprivation of many, if not all, decision-making powers, the mechanism is viewed by many professionals as the intervention of last resort. Guardianship of the elderly has become a topic of much concern in the past decade due to the growing numbers of elderly in our population.

Data presented to the Senate Special Committee on Aging state that by the year 2030, twenty-one (21) percent of the U.S. population will be age 65 or over. Of that 64.5 million Americans, thirty million will be over the age of 75. At the beginning of this century, less than one in ten Americans was 55 or older, and one in twenty-five was 65 or older. By 1985, the population over 55 was twenty-one percent and those 65 or older was twelve percent. Those Americans 85 or older comprise one of the fastest growing age groups in this nation. Between 1980 and 2020, this group will triple in size and by 2050 will be seven times as large, constituting over 16 million Americans (U.S. Senate, 1987).

How our system will judge who is and is not competent, where they will be domiciled, who will manage their assets, and who will make consenting decisions on their behalf are issues of great import and scholarly debate. Even a preliminary review of current literature on the subject of guardianship (public or private) reveals a variety of themes that have generated professional concern. Among them are the issues of: involuntary commitment and civil rights (Alexander, 1975, 1977: Schmidt, 1981, 1984), due process and judicial reform (Atkinson, 1980: Mitchell, 1978; Schmidt, 1986, 1987), competency evaluation (Baker, 1987: Nolan, 1984), role of the guardian (Schmidt, 1984, 1987: Schmidt, Miller, Peters &

Loewenstein, 1988), the psychological effects of guardianship (Parmelee, 1988), and the extent of need for guardians.

In 1983, one of the first published guardianship needs studies was conducted in Florida by Schmidt and Peters (1987). The Florida study assessed the alleged need for public guardianship via a telephone survey of the state's 74 public receiving facilities, community mental health centers, and clinics; 30 private receiving facilities; 11 Aging and Adult district officers; Developmental Services institutional and residential placements; and six state mental hospitals. Along with basic demographic characteristics and data concerning the extent of physical and psychiatric disability, the survey requested the number of legally incompetent clients with and without guardians served by the facility, and the number of functionally incompetent clients. The latter category was defined as those clients ". . . alleged to meet legal criteria for incompetence, but have not yet been formally adjudicated incompetent" (Schmidt & Peters, 1987:70).

The study found that nearly 3,000 legal incompetents, as well as 6,000 functional incompetents, were in need of guardianship services. Another group of 2,250 clients from Developmental Services was alleged to be in need of guardianship services for a combined total of more than 11,000 clients. Further, Schmidt and Peters reported that these numbers probably undercounted the overall need in Florida. Absent from their survey were data concerning private clients residing in nursing homes and adult congregate living facilities, and those outside of the state service system. Some examples of the latter would include transient groups, clients served by the Federal Government (e.g., the Department of Veterans Affairs), clients who never sought any form of public assistance, and those housed in unlicensed facilities. The authors suggested that obtaining accurate data on nursing home clients alone is more difficult since staff at these facilities are often less knowledgeable concerning a client's legal status (Schmidt & Peters, 1987). Attempting to gather data on such groups as transients, those housed in unlicensed facilities, or those who never applied for social services benefits may be virtually impossible. This Tennessee study is the only assessment conducted statewide in Tennessee, or in any other state, of the need for guardians in the private nursing home population.

METHODOLOGY

This need assessment survey was developed in order to document the existing level of need for guardianship services among elderly residents of Tennessee nursing homes. Originally, homes for the aged and residential homes were included in the survey, but the latter were excluded from the analysis for reasons described below. A list prepared by the State of Tennessee of all licensed facilities was utilized as a mailing list. Unlicensed facilities were excluded for obvious reasons; no means of securing addresses or telephone numbers was available, and unlicensed facilities would be unlikely to respond given the possibility of exposing themselves to possible litigation or closing.

Since the entire "licensed-facility" population was approximately 500 facilities, the whole population was surveyed rather than a sample of those facilities. This decision was made for two reasons. First, it was suspected that return rates would be low since the survey was entirely voluntary. Second, a survey of the entire population was financially feasible.

The survey was conducted in two phases. First, a questionnaire was constructed that solicited information about the number of residents; the number of residents in the age groupings of 60 and under, 61-64, 65-74, and 75 and over; the number of white and nonwhite residents; the number of male and female residents; the number of medicaid eligible residents; the number of residents having only mental disabilities, only physical disabilities, and some combination of physical and mental disabilities; the number of current residents that have already been appointed some form of guardianship services; and the number of current residents perceived to need each of the following but for whom there was not a willing and able family member or friend to serve: limited guardian, conservator of property, conservator of person, representative payee, and power of attorney. Respondents were also asked to rate the degree of difficulty in completing the survey ("much," "some," and "no"), as well as how confident they were regarding the accuracy of the information supplied ("not confident," "doubtful," "hard to say," "somewhat confident," and "very confident"). The questionnaire also included statutory definitions of the type of guardianship services to aid administrators in completing the needs assessment.

Questionnaires were mailed in the Summer of 1988 to each licensed facility appearing in the 1987 state guide, along with a cover letter explaining the purposes of the survey and a self-addressed postage-paid envelope. To facilitate higher response rates, the survey was intentionally designed to obtain only aggregate quantitative data with the unit of analysis being the nursing home. Thus, completing the survey did not violate any confidentiality regulations of the residents or their records, and data could be easily entered into a data base management system (DBASE III).

The second phase of the study involved a follow-up telephone survey in the Summer and Fall of 1988. Any facility that provided incomplete or contradictory information or that did not promptly return the survey was telephoned to solicit the necessary information. At most facilities, the respondent was the social services director, but in some cases, administrators, social workers, nursing directors, or records managers completed the survey and/or received the follow-up telephone calls. In some instances, figures obtained were estimates that represented the respondents' best judgment because relevant information was not contained in client files. Lack of computerized records also prohibited some respondents from reporting precise information regarding clients' legal status since assembling such data would be too time consuming.

With reference to the number of clients with perceived need, as Schmidt and Peters (1987) point out, ". . . nonjudicial assessments of legal incompetence are of course suspect but, in the absence of better information, must necessarily suffice" (p.72). As stated, statutory definitions of various legal statuses were provided to assist respondents. It should be pointed out that although perceptions of incompetency by nursing home staff may not be valid and reliable indicators of actual need of public guardianship services, they are good measures of "need for referral." The role of nursing home staff in the system is not to make legal decisions regarding incompetency and need for public guardianship services, but instead, on a subjective basis, to make referrals to public guardian district agencies for further processing. Of course, if reliable and valid measures of incompetency were available, it would make everyone's job easier. Perhaps one set of measures should be developed for referring agencies (such as nursing homes) that err on the side of referring clients (i.e., have a higher number of false positive ratings of incompetency), and another set of more precise measures should be developed for judges who make formal guardianship decisions. Nevertheless, it is important that residents who are perceived by nursing home staff to be in need of public guardianship services actually be referred to district agencies for evaluation. In this paper, it is those residents that should be referred, but have not been, who constitute unmet need.

A mail survey with telephone follow-up was chosen as the methodology to increase the response rate, minimize costs, to facilitate follow-up questions, and answer any questions administrators might have about the survey, its objectives, or any legal ramifications. Although such a methodology has inherent difficulties, the economic circumstances of this needs assessment warranted its usage.

After the first phase of the study (mail survey), residential homes were excluded from the study because it was discovered that almost all licensed residential homes require their residents to be competent and able. Most do not supply medical services or skilled care services. Most residential home administrators contacted stated that their regulations excluded anyone who was adjudicated or later became adjudicated by the court as incompetent.

One hundred and ninety-four residential homes were eligible at the beginning of the study; thirty-one responded to the initial mail survey. Of these, only eight indicated that a public guardian could be utilized in some capacity, generally as a representative payee. And of these eight homes, six homes had six residents or less. An additional seven homes contended that family members were acting "unofficially" as guardians. The remainder insisted that they would not accept anyone who was incompetent. Telephone inquiries to another 25 residential homes that had not responded to the survey revealed that applicants who needed skilled care or who were incompetent were not accepted. Overall, of the 56 homes with which contact was made, none of the larger homes (20 residents or more) would accept residents needing guardianship services of any kind. Therefore, the administrators themselves indicated that residential homes should not be included in the survey. The researchers concurred with this opinion; consequently these facilities were omitted from the analysis.

Data from the surveys were entered into a data base management system (DBASE III) and transferred to SPSS/PC for statistical analysis. Because the entire population of nursing homes was surveyed, the analysis is descriptive, with frequency distributions, measures of central tendency, and crosstabulations constituting the analysis techniques. The unit of analysis is the nursing home.

FINDINGS

From the time the study was initiated, 14 facilities that were on the original list of eligible facilities closed. With the exclusion of the residential homes as described above, 295 facilities remained eligible for the study. One hundred and twenty-three surveys were received for a response rate of 41.7%. As Table 1 demonstrates, of the 123 valid cases, a total of 12,226 residents are reported as domiciled within the various facilities.

Given that the total number of beds available in these homes is 12,894 according to the state guide of licensed nursing homes, the occupancy rate is 94.8%. While the average number of residents per facility is around 99, the median is 79, the mode 12, and the standard deviation 80, which reflects the wide distribution of size of nursing homes in Tennessee. Females constitute 73% of the reported population with an average of nearly 72 female residents per facility. Conversely, males represent 27% of the reported population. Further, the data reveal that nearly 88% of the residents are white.

The older elderly are substantially represented in Tennessee nursing homes. Around 73% of the total reported population is 75 years of age or older; 15% are 65 to 74 years old; and the remaining 12% are under 65 years of age. Finally, approximately 74% of the residents were eligible for Medicaid reimbursement.

As shown in Table 2, 111 nursing homes provided complete data for the current legal status of their clients. In these homes, 238 out of a total of 10,513 residents, or 2.3%, were reported to have a limited guardian. One-hundred and two, or 1% were reported to have a conservator of property, and 190, or 1.8%, had a conservator of person. Six-hundred and eighty residents of the nursing homes surveyed, or 6.5%, used a power of attorney, whereas 2,136 residents, or 20.3%, used a representative payee. Thus, a total of 3,353 residents, or 31.9%, are currently represented by some form of Tennessee guardianship service.

Table 3 provides information pertaining to the amount of perceived need for public guardianship. There were a total of 10,555 residents in the 113 nursing homes eligible for this section of the survey. Three-hundred and twenty-seven residents, or 3.1%, are perceived by nursing home staff to need a limited guardian. Forty-one, or 0.4% need a conservator of property; 80, or 0.8%, need a conservator of person; 417, or 3.95%, need a representative payee; and 179, or 1.7% are perceived to need someone to have power of attorney. Thus, a total of 1,044 residents, or 9.9%, are perceived to be in need of guardianship services but have no one to perform such duties. Interestingly, 49 facilities (43%) reported that no residents were in need of any form of public guardianship services.

TABLE 1. Mean Number and Percentage of Nursing Home Residents with Particular Demographic Characteristics

Variable	mean	(st. dev.)	Absolute Totals Numbera	(%)
Number of Females	72	(59)	8785	(73%)
Number of Males	27	(24)	3250	(27%)
Number of Whites	87	(61)	10331	(88%)
Number of Nonwhites	12	(33)	1426	(12%)
Aged 64 and Under	12	(9)	1361	(6%)
Aged 65-74	15	(16)	1756	(15%)
Aged 75 and Above	72	(61)	8622	(73%)
Medicaid Eligible	73	(76)	8725	(74%)
Total # of Residents	99	(80)	1226	(100%)

*Absolute numbers for sets of characteristics do not sum to the total 12,226 because of missing data.

TABLE 2. Number of Nursing Home Residents Currently Receiving Guardianship Services in Tennessee[a]

Type of Service	Number	(%)
Limited Guardian	238	(2.3%)
Conservator of Property	102	(1.0%)
Conservator of Person	190	(1.8%)
Representative Payee	2136	(20.3%)
Power of Attorney	680	(6.5%)
Total Receiving Any Service	3353	(31.9%)
Total Number of Residents	10513a	(100.0%)

aTotal number of residents in this table not equal to 12,226 because 12 nursing homes had missing information on this section.

To summarize the univariate data, over two-fifths of the residents of the responding Tennessee nursing homes (42%) were in need of Tennessee guardianship services; 32% were having their needs met at the time of the survey, and 10% had no one to assume such a role so public guardianship services were required. It should be noted that although 74% of the respondents indicated some degree of difficulty in completing the survey, fully 81% stated that they were "somewhat to very" confident that the information they provided was accurate.

Because of the 58% nonresponse rate, it is difficult to determine the overall level of unmet need for public guardianship services in Tennessee nursing homes. If the assumption is made that the nursing homes that returned the surveys are representative of all such homes and that, therefore, 9.9% accurately reflects the percentage of residents in need, then extrapolating to all nursing homes suggests that there are 3,003 out of 30,336 total nursing home residents in Tennessee who are in need of public guardianship services. This total also assumes that the occupancy rate for facilities that did not respond is the same 94.8% as for facilities that did respond.

To assess the degree of representativeness of the sample, all nursing homes were categorized by size (small = 50 beds or less; me-

TABLE 3. Number of Nursing Home Residents with Unmet Need for Guardianship Services in Tennessee[a]

Type of Service	Number	(%)
Limited Guardian	327	(3.01%)
Conservator of Property	41	(0.40%)
Conservator of Person	80	(0.80%)
Representative Payee	417	(3.95%)
Power of Attorney	179	(1.70%)
Total Needing Any Service	1044	(9.90%)
Total Number of Residents	10555a	(100.0%)

aTotal number of residents in this table not equal to 12,226 because 10 nursing homes had missing information on this section.

dium = 51 to 149 beds; and large = 150 beds or more) and location (facilities were defined as urban if they were located in MSA counties; otherwise, they were considered as rural). Table 4 provides response rates by a cross-tabulation of these two variables. Large rural facilities and medium urban facilities had the lowest response rates (33.3% and 35.4% respectively), whereas small urban and small rural facilities had the highest response rates (50% and 52% respectively). Overall, then, the data demonstrate that the sample is reasonably representative of Tennessee nursing homes, at least as measured by these variables.

An additional clue that the responding facilities are reasonably representative of all nursing homes in Tennessee is that, according to the state guide, responding facilities have a total of 12,894 beds and nonresponding facilities, 19,099 beds. Thus, the responding facilities have 40.3% of the total available beds which closely matches the 41.7% response rate.

Breakdowns of mean levels of current guardianship usage and unmet need were also done by size and location to determine if there was more need in large, urban facilities. Literature on social networks of the elderly indicates that urban elderly are more likely

TABLE 4. Cross-Tabulation of Size of Facility by Location, with Associated Response Rates

Size	Location								
	Rural			Urban			Total		
	Number	(%)	[Resp.] [Rate]	Number	(%)	[Resp.] [Rate]	Number	(%)	[Resp.] [Rate]
Small (< 51 Beds)	12	(19%)	[52%]	13	(21%)	[50%]	25	(20%)	[51%]
Medium (51-149 Beds)	44	(71%)	[43.6%]	29	(48%)	[35.4%]	73	(59%)	[39.9%]
Large (150+ Beds)	6	(10%)	[33.3%]	19	(31%)	[42.2%]	25	(20%)	[39.7%]
Total	62	(50%)	[43.7%]	61	(50%)	[39.9%]	123	(100%)	[41.7%]

to be socially isolated (Coward & Smith, 1982, Youmans, 1977) and, hypothetically, they may be more likely to require public guardianship services. The cross-tabulation of size of facility by urban-rural status is shown in Table 4, along with associated response rates, whereas the breakdowns mentioned above are given in Table 5.

Sixty-one of the 123 homes that responded to the survey are urban, and 62 are rural. Twenty-five (20.3%) are categorized as small nursing homes, 73 (59.3%) as medium, and 25 (20.3%) as large. As Table 4 indicates, urban nursing homes are more likely to be large, with 31% of homes being so designated as compared to 10% of rural homes being categorized as large. Seventy-one percent of rural homes are designated as medium size as compared to 48% of urban nursing homes.

Table 5 shows by size and location of nursing home the percentage of residents that currently have someone serving in each of the five legal capacities, as well as the percentage of residents in need of the five Tennessee public guardianship alternatives. Because the entire population was surveyed, the sample is not a probability sample. Therefore, inferential statistics with significance testing are not supported by statistical theory. Accordingly, the reader should examine the mean percentages in a straightforward manner. Nevertheless, if the sample had been a probability sample, only one comparison (the percentage in urban and rural nursing homes having limited guardians) would be significant at the .05 significance level.

The overall patterns are as follow: urban nursing homes have slightly more residents currently using a guardian and also have slightly more residents in need of public guardianship services. Urban residents are slightly more likely to have a limited guardian, to have someone using power of attorney, and to be in need of a limited guardian or a conservator of property or person. Rural residents are slightly more likely to have someone serving as representative payee and conservator of property or person, and to be in need of someone to serve as representative payee or to use a power of attorney.

Regarding the effects of size of facility, the data show that the smaller the facility the greater the percentage of current residents who have all forms of guardianship services, with the exception of representative payee. Large facilities are more likely to have larger

TABLE 5. Percentage of Residents Currently Served by a Guardian and Percentage in Need of a Public Guardian by Size and by Location

% of Residents with:	Size			Location		
	Small	Medium	Large	Rural	Urban	Total
Limited Guardian	10.4	3.4	1.6	1.3	8.3	4.6
Conserv. of Property	1.5	1.1	.7	1.2	1.0	1.1
Conserv. of Person	2.2	2.0	1.6	2.3	1.7	2.0
Rep. Payee	15.9	19.4	23.9	23.0	15.7	19.4
Power of Attorney	10.1	8.9	5.8	7.4	9.9	8.6
Total	40.1	34.8	33.6	35.2	36.6	35.6

% of Residents in need of:	Size			Location		
	Small	Medium	Large	Rural	Urban	Total
Limited Guardian	2.9	3.2	3.1	2.0	4.4	3.1
Conserv. of Property	2.1	.1	.7	.1	1.2	.6
Conserv. of Person	.2	.8	.6	.4	1.0	.7
Rep. Payee	2.4	3.6	5.2	4.0	3.2	3.6
Power of Attorney	.5	1.7	1.7	2.1	.8	1.5
Total	8.2	9.4	11.3	8.6	10.6	

percentages of residents using a representative payee. Pertaining to need for public guardianship, larger facilities appear to have more unmet need, primarily because their staff reported a greater need for public guardians to serve as representative payees and to accept power of attorney. All in all, then, the effects of size and location of nursing home were minimal.

CONCLUSION AND DISCUSSION

Even though the percentage of nursing home residents needing public guardianship services is seemingly small, this study has documented that at least 1,044 residents are perceived to require such services. This number is alarmingly high, even though it is an underestimate since 58% of the nursing homes did not respond to the survey. These 1,044 potential clients, if provided with public guardianship program service, would immediately overload the statewide public guardianship program currently administered by the Tennessee Commission on Aging. As noted in the introduction, data obtained from the Commission indicate that 215 total clients were being served by the program during the quarter of October-December 1988. One-hundred and seventeen required full guardianship, the remaining 98 required alternative services with the following: limited guardianship (18); representative payee/legal custodian (54); guardian ad litem (13); and power of attorney (13) (Schmidt & Heckert, 1989). Since potential wards are referred to the public guardian program district agencies by various agents, including family members, nursing home staff, hospital staff, adult protective services, attorneys, and other interested persons, it is curious that so many nursing home residents with unmet need have not been referred to this program. At the least, those 1,044 residents with perceived need should be referred to the public guardianship district agencies.

Another interesting concern is the issue of conflict of interest. Many of the nursing homes responding to the survey indicated that the facility or its administrator functioned as representative payee for a large number of its clients. In some cases, twenty-five (25) or more residents were represented by the facility. Yet, many of the nursing home respondents did not perceive a need for an external monitor (such as a public guardian) to oversee or assume these responsibilities. In fact, many facilities that did not complete the survey frequently reported that workload and/or time constraints prevented them from doing so. Delegating these duties to someone outside the facility, appointed by the state, might serve both parties well. While this should not be construed as evidence of abuse or of intent to defraud clients of their funds, the introduction of a third party could at least reduce the potential and/or appearance of conflict of interest. None of the above residents were included in the category of residents with perceived need, but if they were included that figure would come closer to 1,500 clients. Reducing potential conflict of interest would appear to be in the best interests of both the facility and the governmental agencies that oversee licensure and disbursement of governmental funds.

Finally, the state of record keeping that exists in many Tennessee nursing homes is a concern. The most frequently cited reasons for not completing the survey were time constraints, workload, and insufficient data. In the latter case, many facilities could not state if a client had or had not been adjudicated by a court, what form of guardianship had been imposed, or even who the legal guardian was. A common example reported would be: ". . . a family member is acting 'unofficially' as a guardian but our records don't indicate who they are. . . ." One can only surmise the confusion that must exist if that client should become acutely ill and require invasive medical/surgical intervention. Attempting to discover the proper party to sign a consent/release form could delay necessary treatment. Thus, computerization of client records would be valuable to both the client and the facility for reasons other than research. Over the last ten years, computers have become a staple of the small business community, as well as the patient care industry. While the state might be reluctant to mandate computerized management information systems for the nursing home industry, it might be appropriate for the state to mandate that facilities maintain records about the legal status of all residents of licensed facilities, along with the names and relationships of guardians and what form of protective services has been imposed. Further, nursing homes should report the names of any clients who need referral for assessing competency and/or protective services to public guardian agencies.

REFERENCES

Alexander, G. (1975). Forward: Life, liberty and property rights for the elderly. *Arizona Law Review*, *17*, 267-274.

Alexander, G. (1977). On being imposed upon by artful or designing persons—the California experience with the involuntary placement of the aged. *San Diego Law Review*, *14*, 1083-1099.

Atkinson, G. 1980, June. Towards a due process perspective in conservatorship proceedings for the aged. *Journal of Family Law*, *18*, 819-845.

Baker, F. (1987). Competent for what? *Journal of the National Medical Association*, *79*, 715-720.

Coward, R. & Smith, W. (1982). Families in rural society. In D. Dillman & D. Hobbs (Eds.). *Rural society in the U.S.: Issues for the 1980's* (pp. 77-84). Boulder, Co: Westview Press.

Langen, W. (1978). Protecting the interests of the ward. *Law and Human Behavior*, *2*, 267-283.

Mitchell, A. (1978). Involuntary guardianship for incompetents: A strategy for legal services advocates. *Clearinghouse Review*, *12*, 451-468.

Nolan, B. (1984). Functional evaluation of the elderly in guardianship proceedings. *Law, Medicine and Health Care*, *12*, 210-218.

Parmelee, P. (1980). Do we deal competently with incompetence? *Law and Politics Quarterly*, 397-419.

Schmidt, W. (1981). Guardianship of the elderly in Florida. *Florida Bar Journal*, *55*, 189-195.

Schmidt, W. (1984). The evolution of a public guardianship program. *The Journal of Psychiatry and Law*, *12*, 349-372.

Schmidt, W. (1986). Adult protective services and the therapeutic state. *Law and Psychology Review*, *10*, 101-121.

Schmidt, W. (1987). Recommended judicial practices in guardianship proceedings for the elderly. *The Florida Bar Journal*, *61*, 35-39.

Schmidt, W., & Heckert, A. (1989). *National guardianship census and empirical comparison of guardianship and alternatives to guardianship.* (Unpublished paper, Memphis State University).

Schmidt, W., Miller, K., Peters, R., & Loewentstein, D. (1988). A descriptive analysis of professional and volunteer programs for the delivery of public guardianship services. *Probate Law Journal*, *8*, 125-156.

Schmidt, W. & Peters, R. (1987). Legal incompetents' need for guardians in Florida. *Bulletin of the Academy of Psychiatry and Law*, *15*, 69-82.

U.S. Senate. (1987). Special Committee on Aging. *Development in Aging*. 100th Cong., 1st Sess., Washington, D.C.: GPO, v. 3.

Youmans, E. (1977). Rural aged. *Annals of the American Academy of Political and Social Science 429*, 81-91.

Social Contract, Communities and Guardians

Erich H. Loewy, MD

SUMMARY. This paper examines the way that different notions of social contract and community change the way in which we can look at the obligations guardians have to their charges. A brief analysis of the underpinnings of autonomy based (minimalist) and beneficence based (non-minimalist) ethics is given and the consequences of such points of view are scrutinized. This paper argues that the minimalist ethic is flawed in theory as well as practice. The consequences for guardians of these theories is sketched.

Issues of guardianship, to be properly understood, must be examined in the larger context of societal structure. Guardianship, whether institutional guardianship or individual guardianship, imposes a heavy obligation on the guardian. In the relationship of parents to children we take this for granted. Biological factors, social pressures and, above all, ongoing association usually (but, regrettably by no means always) enables a bilateral and evolving relationship to which mutual love and trust are central. Furthermore, children normally bond, grow up and become mature self-determining adults in the embrace of a family so that the parent child relationship from the very beginning has a quite different flavor than adult guardianship. Here there is usually no hope that the relationship will mature, and often relationships are of a more formal kind

---

Erich H. Loewy is Associate Professor of Medicine at the University of Illinois College of Medicine at Peoria, Box 1649, Peoria, IL 61656 and Associate Professor of Humanities (Ethics) at the University of Illinois at Chicago.

The issues raised here are detailed in Loewy, E.H.: *Suffering and the Beneficent Community: Beyond Libertarianism*. Albany, NY: SUNY Press; 1990 (forthcoming).

especially when guardians are either institutional or court appointed. In such instances, the duties of guardianship are ultimately discharged by persons whose relationship to the person is formal: they are "case-workers" assigned to the case. This is a particularly difficult task since "case-workers" rarely knew such patients before they became "cases." Since case-workers are the employees of institutions and, furthermore, since such case-workers are very often if not almost routinely overworked, there is a strong temptation to exercise guardianship by strictly following rules and regulations rather than by exercising autonomous judgments within the framework of such rules and regulations. Although easier than formulating individualized difficult judgments, the mindless application of rules and regulations, like the mindless application of principles when applying ethics, scuttles the moral enterprise which relies on compassion, discernment and disgression.[1,2]

The problems encountered by guardians in dealing with their wards are a reflection of the tension between individual and communal interests, autonomy and beneficence. Such a tension, furthermore, plays itself out in a particular communal context underwritten by specific and often unenunciated values and feelings depending on a prior vision of social contract and community. A society which has little value for beneficence will see the role of guardians quite differently than will one which places on beneficence a higher value.

The ways in which we view our ethical obligations depend upon a number of factors. Principal among these is the way we feel social contract originated and exists today. Attitudes towards community, its structure and how solidarity in such communities can be brought about emerge from the way we view social contract. In turn, the way we view community (whether a community in which beneficent duties are minimal or not) determines our attitudes towards mutual obligation.

This paper will argue against a minimalist community: one in which beneficence has little moral standing and in which the safeguarding of individual autonomy is ethically of primary importance. It will (1) review the Hobbesian vision of social contract (based on mutual terror and eventuating in the Nozickian notion of an entirely autonomy based ethic), contrast it with more generous models and show how our notion of community—as well as solidarity—emerges from a prior assumption about the nature of social contract; (2) show that a minimalist ethic (like that of Nozick and Engelhardt) is flawed in principle as well as in practice and that, therefore, beneficence inevitably enters the moral equation; and (3) present a dialectic concept of autonomy (generally in agreement with Pellegrino's and Thomasma's view which sees a high regard for autonomy as necessarily emerging from beneficence) and make the point that too much emphasis on autonomy is often a "cop-out": a "Pontius Pilate act" allowing us to conveniently wash our hands of the matter and eventually resulting in poverty, want and neglect. On the other hand, we will show that unbridled beneficence can result in the crasser forms of paternalism and can become merely the beneficence of the Gulag. Finally I want to draw some practical conclusions for our society from such considerations, conclusions which inevitably involve issues of great importance to notions of guardianship.

SOCIAL CONTRACT, COMMUNITY AND OBLIGATION

The existence of social contract will be assumed rather than argued for. If one means by social contract an association of persons coming together in order to govern themselves one is talking of a somewhat different matter. Government may be the result of social contract but not all or even most governments are. Social contract, while it may be used more narrowly to support various forms of government, indeed is a far richer concept then merely the concept underwriting government: it implies all the tacit agreements ultimately enabling communal life. A form of social contract in that sense underpins all associations and, in turn, a wider social contract enables the formation of such associations in the first place.[3-5]

Social contract implies those unspoken, tacit assumptions which meld people together and which allow them to exist as associations. It consists, in other words, of those things which "go without saying."[6] A collective or community is not possible without such fundamental and quite tacit understandings. Law emerges from social contract and, in due time, and in turn, may influence the evolution of the way we look at social contract and obligation. The relationship, eventually, is reciprocal but law is ontologically subsequent and not prior to the contract itself. Life without a social contract—life without such tacit understandings whatever they might be in the particular—would be unimaginable.

Notions of social contract are not new. The fact of social contract itself, as distinct from governmental contract, is so very evident and obvious that it may often be missed even when it is tacitly assumed. The idea of social contract (at least as it is heard by modern ears) carries with it a notion of equality. As the 17th century English Leveller Col. Rainsborough wrote:

> Really, I think that the poorest he that is in England has a life to live as the greatest he: and, therefore, truly Sir I think it's clear that every man . . . ought first by his own consent to put himself under that government. . . .[6]

About the same time, Hobbes vigorously argued for rather than merely tacitly assumed the first modern notion of social contract. Hobbes saw original man as living in a "state of nature" and his life as inevitably "solitary, nasty, brutish and short."[7] Persons lived in fear and terror of each other and it was this fear and terror which gave rise to the original contract. If fear of each other could be reduced and men could be reasonably free of fear from their fellows a more productive life could result. And so, in the original state of nature, men came out from behind their tree or rock to covenant with each other and, ultimately, to reach a compact predicated merely on mutual non-harm. Coming to another's aid was not part of the bargain.

There are other ways of thinking about social contract. Locke saw social contract as being forged among equally free men united by an evolving trust rather than as a contract based merely on mutual fear. Executing (and formulating) the laws is the duty of the individual rather than merely the function of an omnipotent sovereign.[8] Rousseau took this entire concept a good deal further. For him, the "state of nature" was a somewhat more primitive one than was Locke's (Locke's state, curiously enough, already included such notions as private property and an economy) but for Rousseau primitive life was more benign and not endowed with the same savageness as it had been for Hobbes. Primitive man was essentially an isolated and amoral being although already possessed of a "natural sense of pity." In Rousseau's view, social structure originates in the general will which emerges through the establishment of civil associations and is "constant, incorruptible and pure."[9] Social structure created individual morality by transforming the amoral and animal-like state of nature.[9] To Rousseau, just as for Hobbes the social contract could occur only after some development of the primitive state had occurred. Prior to the possibility of a social contract human character had to be changed.

As Rousseau envisioned social contract, individuals can only be properly seen within the nexus of their social connections. Associations of this sort, just as is the case with Locke, do far more than merely prevent mutual harm: they actively promote the "good," here seen as a social "good" incomprehensible outside the social nexus. To Rousseau the condition of "civilized man" in which poverty and injustice were the rule, violated the original contract and ran counter to the general will. A return to a more basic way of life prior to corruption, was to be desired.

To Hobbes, solidarity in a community required only the realization that others would be prevented from doing one harm; beneficence was not needed. Solidarity to Locke depended on mutual trust and to Rousseau solidarity was a function of a social nexus resulting in the general will and actively promoting social good. Solidarity to Rousseau was endangered by modern, corrupted conditions gone astray.

One can, however, think of social contract in other ways.[10,11] Instead of seeing communities formed only by contracting individuals, such a notion may be denied altogether. Rather, persons can be seen as being born into family and tribal groups and thus as emerging in communities. A social contract, in such a view, is a necessary part of any such group from the very start. "Contracts," rather than being formed in terror, are formed in the close embrace of a family, tribe or like association. A much more complex and interactive model emerges and such a model, rather than being based on terror is based on bonds of mutual love, trust, needs and, inescapably, bio-social interdependence. As children grow up they may begin to fear others, may, in fact, be in terror of others from other tribes or associations. But their initial social contract is a tacit one and is one made implicitly with those with whom they bonded and who nurtured and sustained them. Warmth and fellowship, therefore, are part of such an initial contract. The infant's sense of selfhood and its fledgling autonomy emerges in the embrace of beneficence.

Families and tribes in turn may discover the need for larger communal living and may then covenant with other tribes. Of course, the notion of mutual non-harm is critical: it is a necessary but far from sufficient condition for covenant. The very notion of covenanting and of non-harm must be seen as underwritten by trust if it is to come about in the first place or if it is to endure in the final analysis.[12] Without trust, men would be unlikely to emerge from behind their tree or rock to covenant. Unless there is mutual trust, man cannot even think of "covenanting together"; unless there is mutual need (of which the need for protection from harm by possible others in the group is only a small part), no impulse for entering such associations exists. Trust, in turn, presupposes that, at the very least, our fellows care about our welfare and, where possible, are willing to come to our aid. A feeling of beneficence, then, is basic to such a theory.[11] Solidarity, in such communities, is not only a function of being left alone and not harmed; it is secured, likewise, by reliance on mutual good will and beneficence. Modern societies could, if they did not surrender to crass individualism and greed, evolve without returning to an impossible to imagine "primitive" state.

The critical influence which viewpoints of social contract have on the way we envision community is obvious. When we feel obligated not to harm another even when we are most angry or, on the other hand, feel obliged to help another in need or distress, we base these feelings on a more general viewpoint of social contract. If we think that our initial coming together was grounded merely in mutual terror and that refraining from harming each other was the necessary as well as the sufficient condition for such a contract, we will see communities fashioned on such a model. On the other hand, if we see such a contract as not only based on terror but assume bonds of mutual love, trust, needs and bio-social interdependence, a quite different viewpoint of community will emerge. The obligations we assume towards others in the community as well as towards the community itself, is directly linked to the way we see community being fashioned. Solidarity is what makes communities cohesive and solidarity is felt because the persons in community feel reasonably satisfied with their lot. The degree of satisfaction members feel is intimately linked with the solidarity communities will develop.

Examining the Minimalist Ethic

We shall argue that the minimalist ethic (like that of Nozick and Engelhardt) is flawed in principle as well as in practice and that, therefore, beneficence inevitably enters the moral equation.

If we accept a Hobbesian view of social contract, a minimalist community emerges. Communities founded on a contract promising only mutual non-harm and nothing else are minialist communities: communities in which freedom and autonomy are absolutes. Freedom and autonomy (as long as no explicit harm comes to one's fellow by the exercise of freedom and autonomy) are conditions and not values of the moral life. Respect for autonomy and protection of autonomy is what the ethical life is all about. Beneficence, caring, charity, all are non-moral obligations. As envisioned by Nozick (and in the field of medical ethics by Engelhardt) obligations are of two sorts: (1) those of mutual non-harm (and, therefore, those respecting absolute freedom except as the exercise of such freedom would explicitly limit the autonomy of another); and (2) those freely assumed by explicit mutual contract. Beneficence is, perhaps, a most desirable sentiment but it carries no moral weight except as it may be part of particular moral enclaves. Such moral enclaves may internally freely exact obligations of beneficence as a condition of membership but their peculiar points of view have force only within the enclave itself. It is difficult to see why beneficence is even a desirable sentiment. Beneficence no longer has moral weight but rather has an almost aesthetic value. Like raspberry sherbet or the music of Mozart, it may appeal to some but not to others. Its appeal is, from a moral point of view, idiosyncratic and purely volitional. Freely entered contracts in which both parties understand the terms must be allowed and strictly enforced no matter what their stipulations. According to libertarians, pluralist communities must constitute themselves in this fashion or remain forever in conflict. No one's moral point of view can be enforced upon all; all members are free to dissent and to go their own way except when it comes to directly injuring another or to violating freely entered, explicit and mutually understood contracts.[13,14]

The consequences of looking at communities in this fashion are communities in which laws limit private actions only insofar as such actions directly and immediately bring injury to another. Even here, certain actions, such as dueling, though clearly injurious, might be allowable. Societies of this sort give entrepreneurialism a free hand. Taxes can be imposed only insofar as the money was needed to insure the liberty of all citizens. It is the function of the State to insure maximal personal liberty for all, limited only by everyone's obligation not to infringe the liberty of their fellow man. Taxes to maintain police power sufficient to this end would be one of the few legitimate forms of taxation. Money from the wealthy for the benefit of the poor can be obtained only through voluntary contributions. The licensing of health professionals is not morally possible and drug or pure food laws, cannot be made or enforced. Physicians become "bureaucrats of health," vending machines who supply patients with whatever patients may want regardless of the physician's own moral point of view provided only that doing so is legal and provided the patient promptly pays the stipulated sum. Guardianship, if it existed at all, is administered by persons hired to oversee those incapable of overseeing themselves in order to enforce mutual non-harm. Beneficence towards the person guarded by the guardian, doing things to actively promote good rather than merely preventing harm, is not an expected obligation though it might well be a thing which for non-moral reasons a guardian might choose to do. The supposed solidarity (and, therefore, the peacefulness) of such communities emerges purely from the single obligation not to do each other harm. It is the necessary cement of such communities and, according to such a philosophy, it is held also to be sufficient.

When communities assume freedom as an absolute they are unable to balance freedom with other obligations and, therefore, lose flexibility. Such communities are often unable to evolve and grow. When communities of this sort are threatened by intolerable danger (say, an epidemic) and find that to counter the danger some restriction of personal liberties seem in order they lack flexibility: they cannot trade freedom and beneficence as values and cannot reach compromises. Dangers to the community cannot be reduced by compromising freedom in any way: autonomy is absolute and cannot be attenuated. When non-flexible communities finally violate their principles, as they are likely to do when an ongoing threat becomes overwhelming, such communities may well become much more oppressive than would flexible cmmunities able to adapt themselves to changing circumstances. Crass individualism easily lends itself to a dominance of the weak by the strong and of the poor by the rich.[15] Tyranny can easily arrive in the Trojan horse of absolute freedom.[16,17]

Communities can be seen as fashioned in other ways. If one adopts a view of social contract which denies the ontological priority of individuals (or which simply shrugs off the question as unanswerable and irrelevant) and sees social contract as an evolving one necessitated by mutual needs, love, trust, and bio-social interdependence, an initial contract necessitating beneficence clearly emerges. Such communities will not make freedom or anything else an absolute condition but, rather, will be able to adjust their values and formulate their policies in a dynamic fashion. When freedom is not an absolute condition of the moral life but rather one of its esteemed values, a dialectic between individual autonomy and communal needs emerges. Such a dialectic is similar to an Aristotelian striving for the mean. Beneficence, in such a community, may well be held to be a condition prior to respecting autonomy: one cannot, as Pellegrino and Thomasma have so clearly pointed out, be truly beneficent to anyone without having a high regard for that person's wishes and points of view.[18] A respect for autonomy clearly emerges from a beneficence based ethic; the obverse — that a regard for beneficence of necessity emerges from an autonomy based ethic — is clearly not the case.

Communities built on a beneficent model are communities in which laws could limit private actions when such limitations clearly benefit the values held by the community. Clearly injurious actions, such as dueling, can be proscribed if a sufficient number of the members of community feel the proscribed action to be inconsistent with its ideals. Societies of this sort are apt to limit crass entrepreneurialism when it is seen to interfere with the communities welfare. Taxes can be imposed on all citizens, if imposing such taxes is seen as necessary for promoting the welfare of all members. Taxing the wealthy for the benefit of the truly poor and guaranteeing minimal subsistance needs to all members, is apt to become the order of the day. Health professionals can be licensed and drug or pure food laws and other laws to promote the welfare and safety of the citizenry can be made and enforced. Physicians now are more than merely "bureaucrats of health." No longer are they seen and see themselves merely as vending machines who supply patients with whatever patients may want regardless of the physician's own peculiar moral point of view. Their own moral viewpoint matters and while they are not entitled to force their viewpoint down the patient's throat neither are they obligated to provide services they themselves may feel professionally uncalled for or, in their own peculiar view, feel to be immoral. The relationship of health professionals to their charges now is one of mutual trust, and beneficence has a legitimate, and perhaps a central, moral role. Guardianship, necessary for those in the community unable to make their own decisions, is more than merely an act of protecting persons from possible harm by others. Guardians are not here merely to blindly enforce bureaucratic rules. Beneficence towards the person guarded by the guardian in a beneficent community, is a communal norm and doing things to actively promote good rather than merely prevent harm, is an expected obligation. The solidarity (and, therefore, the peacefulness) of such communities can be seen to emerge from an interplay of forces based on an initial social contract firmly grounded in mutual needs, love, trust, and bio-social interdependence. Beneficence, as well as the respect for autonomy which must go with it, is the necessary cement of such communities and, according to this philosophy, beneficence and all that flows from it is held to be a necessary condition of the moral life. When communities balance and reassess their values in an ongoing fashion, communities maintain flexibility. Such communities can evolve and grow. As circumstances change, communities will feel that they can adapt their particular behavior to current needs. Not free to savage their member's autonomy at will, they can, nevertheless, not overlook the welfare, rather than merely the opportunity for freedom, of all.

The claim that a minimalist ethic based on an initial contract forged merely in terror is flawed in principle and flawed, as well as reprehensible, in practice can be shown to be true. In principle, as I have argued, the idea that any association or covenant could be founded merely on mutual terror and on nothing else seems unlikely. Sitting down at a table (or coming out from behind a rock or tree) in order to forge a covenant requires a far richer soil than the soil of fear and terror. Not that fear of one another may not be a legitimate ingredient; but fear alone, while it may play a role in motivating us, does not supply a sufficient condition for us to leave the safety of our own lines. A belief, however minimal, that others can, however little, be trusted to keep an agreement (that, in other words, they will not stab us in the back at the first opportunity) is basic. There is no reason, furthermore, to believe that human beings raised in the embrace of a family would not have a good deal of trust towards their initial community, a feeling of trust inevitably necessary for widening the covenant. The impetus for widening such a covenant originates in a perception of mutual needs, love, and trust underwritten by an inevitable bio-social interdependence. To be established or maintained, solidarity grounded in satisfaction with the community necessitates more than an implied protection from a feared other. It is difficult to see, even in theory, how communities grounded merely in terror of one another could ever come about or how they could grow and sustain themselves.

In practice, communities of this sort have never existed and do not exist today. No nation, even the most crassly capitalist, does not at the very least acknowledge, however minimal obligations of beneficence. In so doing, nations tax the wealthy for the benefit of the poor even when they allow gaping loopholes and even when the benefit to the poor is grudging and grossly insufficient. At the very least, communities pay lip service to beneficent obligations. What is at issue in practice is not the moral status of beneficence but rather the extent to which beneficence should be thrown into the balance. Allowing one's neighbor to starve while throwing away good food would seem, to most of us, to be a reprehensible thing. Equally, societies which needlessly allow some to starve, freeze or go without medical care while others live in opulence or squander enormous wealth does not accord with the vision of social justice most of us would lay claim to.

Guardianship in societies which do more than pay lip service to beneficence as a moral obligation is undoubtedly a far more difficult task than would be guardianship in societies where only the performance of a minimal duty would be expected. But it is also, on human terms, a far more satisfying task. Good guardians, like good parents or good families, must do far more than merely protect their charges against overt harm and they cannot simply use an appeal to autonomy as an excuse for neglecting beneficence and care.

Autonomy and Beneficence Balanced

The pendulum in the United States has swung heavily in favour of autonomy. Capitalist societies of necessity emphasize autonomy and downplay beneficence except as a personal and individual avocation (the "thousand points of light" are an example). In such societies individual "rights" are emphasized and more basic human needs go begging. Access must be free and open to all but enabling access (as contrasted to not interfering with access) is not seen to be a pressing communal obligation. Beneficence, while lip-service is paid to it and while it is much praised when it comes from private initiative, is not viewed as a potent ethical obligation of the community. This is expressed in the way in which we fund guardianship as well as when we look at the status of our poor, our elderly and, often, our young.

The balance between autonomy and beneficence (between, in different words, individual rights and communal obligations) is a balancing act. There is no substantial difference between seeing respect for autonomy emerging from a beneficent based ethic as Pellegrino and Thomasma do,[18] and seeing an ongoing dialectic between the two from which the communal ethos emerges.[6] Neither point of view sees duties of beneficence or obligations to respect autonomy as sufficient; both points of view see duties of beneficence and obligations to respect autonomy as necessary. Justice, in the minimalist ethic, consists of non-interference; in a broader based ethic, justice is a far richer and far more complicated notion.

Doing justice by our wards, in the context of a minimalist ethic, requires us to guard them from harm but does not enjoin us to actively promote their good. A broader based ethic requires active facilitation of the good beyond what is required to shield such persons from harm.

If we accept that an ethic which makes of autonomy and freedom an absolute, a condition rather than a value of the moral life that is both theoretically and practically seriously flawed, there remains a working out of the particulars of the balance between autonomy and beneficence: in the parlance of Pellegrino and Thomasma, the extent to which a respect for autonomy ought properly to emerge from a beneficent ethic and in the dialectic model the extent to which communal and individual obligations and interests ought to be balanced. If one hopes for a sure-fire recipe either from the point of view which sees an ongoing dialectic between autonomy and beneficence or from the point of view which sees a respect for autonomy necessarily emerging from beneficence, one hopes in vain. Sure-fire recipes are inflexible, and the very essence of both points of view is flexibility. We learn from our mistakes, we consider the context and while we adapt our policy to the prevalent communal ethos we do not consider such an ethos as fixed and immutable.

The tension between these two ethical obligations, the tension between the individual and the community of which the individual is a part, is a dynamic one. Some communities will, at a particular time, swing in one, some in another direction. In America today, the pendulum has swung greatly to the side of autonomy. Beneficence is paid lip-service to but effective signs of social beneficence go begging. Between 1977 and 1988 the income of the lowest 40% of the population has dropped, that of the lowest 10% by 10.5%; simultaneously, the income of the top 10% has increased by 27.4% and that of the top 1% by 74.2%.[19] At the same time, the number of persons without insurance for medical care (most of whom are incapable of paying for their own care) has risen to 37 million or 18% of the population.[20] Children go without immunization or well-baby care (let alone often without adequate nutrition), many pregnant women are without prenatal care and the elderly, while their physician fees and hospital bills are partly covered often are unable to buy the medicines prescribed or follow the regimen outlined.

The aim of any society is, of course, first of all to have peace. Without that, nothing else can be accomplished. Minimalists will argue that peace cannot be achieved unless autonomy is taken as the necessary and sufficient condition of a communal ethos. Unless that is the case, they argue, a pluralist society will inevitably be at war. Only if all are left to do as they will, hedged in only by duties of mutual non-harm, can peace be assured. History, however, teaches otherwise. When the material needs of some members are not met while other members openly revel in their enjoyment of opulent luxuries, solidarity is shattered, peace vanishes and, inevitably, revolutions result. When the homeless are left to wander the streets, the hungry are left unfed and the sick are without medical care, a situation practically inimical to peace results and only the arms of a powerful state can prevent open warfare. And that not forever.

Some not only excuse but, in fact, laud an autonomy based ethic and the resulting entrepreneurial system not only for the community but even and quite specifically for health-care.[21] Morality, in that point of view, can be built around an entrepreneurial system and emerges from it. The entrepreneurial system is said to be a new and viable basis for medical morality as, apparently, it is held to be for morality generally. This is a curious point of view. Entrepreneurialism, no matter how or what one may think of it, is imbedded in a communal ethos and follows from a communally acknowledged morality. To claim that communal morality can derive from entrepreneurialism rather than the converse is to turn the pyramid on its head.[22] Arguing that the ground of such a morality is autonomy as an absolute and that entrepreneurialism is only the inevitable result of such a grounding, improves such a position only slightly. Autonomy as an absolute is, as I have shown, flawed not only in its ontological theory but likewise is not in fact a grounding for any known and viable communal ethos. At any rate, an autonomy based entrepreneurial system is a cold system in which patient and doctor are obligated to each other by explicit contract and by nothing else. Transposing this to guardianship would make the guardian responsible to do whatever it is he/she had been hired for and nought else. Rules and regulations are to be applied in an almost Newtonian fashion the way the "law is applied to circumstances."

The preeminence which in the United States is currently assigned to freedom and autonomy has been one of the causes for what many perceive as a system lacking in social justice. Individual freedoms are lauded and, indeed, when we speak of "human rights" in the United States today we invariably are speaking of such individual freedoms. And yet, individual freedoms outside a system of social justice which at the very least secures basic human necessities is a cynical joke. By themselves individual rights do not adequately describe the concept of "human rights" if by human rights we mean those rights society secures to us so that meaningful existence can be enjoyed. Freedom of speech or of assembly is quite meaningless to someone starving or freezing to death. Social justice or a fair share of the necessities of life is a precondition for the enjoyment of those things we, in this country, call human rights.[11,23] Without social justice, with an ethic distorted badly towards the side of autonomy at the expense of beneficence and community, one ends up with poverty, hunger, and homelessness.

A beneficent ethic carried to extremes is likewise not without severe dangers. It is easy to deny others their rightful choice, to claim that we know better what is good for them than they do and to end up with a crassly paternalistic system. Patients who are not consulted about their care or whose wishes are ignored are an example. On a societal level, governments may take on this task deciding that certain things are and are not good to know, read or hear. Persons, for their own good or for the benefit of the community, may be silenced or removed from the community. Guardianship may then eventuate into a crass paternalism in which the guardian not only simply overrides any residual autonomy the ward may legitimately have but by so doing actually diminishes the ward's already diminished sense of autonomy still further. On a societal level, an overriding concern for beneficence too easily may end up in the Gulag.

PRACTICAL CONCLUSIONS

When guardians deal with their charges, a fine balance is needed. By definition, persons needing a guardian are incapable of making at least some important autonomous choices. Autonomy, however, is not an all or nothing thing. Biological as well as environmental, social, and cultural factors impose very real constraints on autonomy.[6,25] Some may not be capable of exercising autonomy in some but be quite capable of exercising it in others. Preserving and, where possible, restoring at least some autonomy (educating persons to accept some responsibility for themselves and encouraging them to make autonomous choices) may not only be one of the noblest functions of medicine but, likewise, may be one of the most satisfying things a guardian can do.[26] In truth, when guardians try to be beneficent as regards their charges, a decent respect for those wishes and values their charges can enunciate is of extreme importance. At the same time, there must on the guardians' part be an initial presumption against allowing others, especially others for whom one is responsible, to come to harm.[27]

The community in appointing guardians, whether such guardians are friends, members of the patient's family, or institutional guardians working for the state, has affirmed that the ward is no longer capable of making critical judgments: that he/she is "incompetent" to handle their own affairs. To safeguard the ward, communities have insisted that another make final judgments when it comes to such critical matters. Guardians, when the guardian is not a family member and the institutions for which the specific guardians work, will have to make choices for their patients and will have to speak in their behalf. On the one hand, they must be careful not to superimpose their own vision of what is or what is not "good" on an unwilling (and quite possibly still partly autonomous) patient; on the other hand, they must have a high priority not only to prevent palpable harm but to make immediate choices which ultimately will serve the patient's, as far as possible self-selected, good.

Let me illustrate: a mentally impaired patient who otherwise enjoys life may refuse a vital transfusion of blood or an operation for cancer. The guardian here must be attuned to the patient's values in making an ultimate choice. He or she must balance the patient's immediate biomedical good with what is or can be known about the patient's higher goods.[18] It may be the case that the patient, even when fully functional, had always refused blood or surgery as part of a deeply held and firmly fixed religious or other conviction. On the other hand, it may be the case that the patient refuses because the disease impairs his/her ability to foresee and judge consequences and, therefore, to reason appropriately. Which of these reasons underpins the patient's refusal is critical if the ultimate choice is to be justly and compassionately made. Furthermore, decisions of what and what not to do or to treat should be informed by certain considerations. The acuteness of the threat, the burden of the disease as opposed to the burden of the intervention sought, as well as the capacity of the patient for cooperation and sustained understanding must all be considered.[28] When guardians put primacy on an autonomy ethic, they are apt to follow one of two paths: either blindly follow the patient's wishes regardless of the consequences entailed or (and more likely since they are generally working for institutions) becoming bureaucrats who blindly carry out prescribed rules and unthinkingly apply regulations. When, however, the tension between beneficence and autonomy favors beneficence more or when respect for autonomy emerges from beneficence as the prime consideration, guardians will be inclined to weigh and sift options and to make compassionate choices based on individual considerations. An autonomy based ethic in which guardians are bureaucrats easily becomes a technical occupation in which humanity and compassion are lost.

Institutions all too often solve their grantedly vexing problems by passing blanket rules and regulations which are then applied to specific situations in a "cookie-cutter" fashion. Many states, for example, do not allow "do not resuscitate" decisions to be written or treatment to be limited for any patient who falls under State Guardianship. This produces a blanket "protection" assuring that everyone will get maximal, but not at all necessarily optimal, treatment: all treatment which it is technically possible to give regardless of other considerations. Such a rule forces patients who are wards of the State and who are suffering from terminal illnesses to have their act of dying prolonged. It is a convenient rule: convenient, that is, for the State and, unfortunately, convenient for guardians who, when non-compassionate choices are made for them, need not trouble themselves to make compassionate ones. Individual disgression is no longer the issue: the individual case has long ago been decided by blanket rules and regulations broaching no exceptions or making exceptions extremely difficult to obtain. This, in effect, deprives the powerless of equal protection. Those with the capacity to negotiate are far more likely to die in the way that they see fit and without having their act of dying prolonged than are those who are being "protected."

Rules of this sort are intended as a *prima facie* hedge against the neglect which may, all too often, be visited upon the power—and voiceless. A blanket rule proscribing all "do not resuscitate orders" on wards of the state, however, assumes a strange norm: it assumes that the medical establishment would be likely to neglect such patients rather than assuming that such neglect was the exception and a form of moral malpractice. The presumption underlying this belief is one in which the medical profession, just like society and from society's point of view, therefore, perhaps not unreasonably, is seen as subscribing largely to an autonomy based ethic in which beneficence has a low moral standing. Beneficent obligations force compassionate choices. Physicians as well as guardians may, if an autonomy based ethic is presumed, lose the counsel of beneficence and, therefore, be far more ready to abandon the treatment of patients they consider incapable of making autonomous choices.

If one accepts a minimal community in which obligations of beneficence have no moral force, protecting persons from harm rather than facilitating their good lends itself to judgments in which only the biomedical good is pursued or to judgments which for the sake of convenience fail to make individual judgments about individual cases. After all, patients are "being protected from harm" and harm is defined in terms of the biomedical good which, under normal circumstances, all who seek medical care are apt to pursue. For the guardian, such a stance is far easier. The biomedical good is more easily determined and what can be done is more readily demonstrable than are higher goods (especially in patients who cannot enunciate their feelings and in whom a great deal of time needs to be spent in searching for their world-view).

A vision of social contract, community and morality inclining to an autonomy based ethic will have little time for beneficent considerations. It will grant autonomy as long as it can and shrug its shoulders at the consequences for those who, perhaps, were truly incapable of making such choices. When, however, autonomy is truly lost and a patient has, in fact, become a ward of the state, guardians who subscribe to such an ethic will easily become bureaucrats once again applying rules and regulations rather than making compassionate and often painful decisions.

On a level of daily practice, guardians are bound by rules. I have argued that such rules must be compassionately applied. But that is not enough. Such rules may, in themselves, be severely flawed as, I personally believe, the blanket rule proscribing DNR orders is. Guardians are citizens, members of the very community which enunciated the rules and which, ultimately, hired them. Rousseau speaks of "magistrates" as participating in three functions or "wills": they are (1) individuals whose will seeks its own advantage; (2) "magistrates" whose will is concerned with official functions; and (3) participants in the "general will" which Rousseau sees as sovereign and, ultimately, as legislative.[9] As guardians, a beneficent ethic would counsel the application of compassionate disgression to rules whereas an autonomy based ethic would be satisfied with being "bureaucrats of the commission." As participants in the general will from which the law and the rules emerge, however, guardians must participate in formulating the rules under which they then operate. They are morally compelled to do this, especially since they have by far the greater experience with specific issues and problems. When they are informed by an entirely autonomy based ethic, guardians will be happy to be excellent bureaucrats during working hours, free to pursue their private interests when not working for the state. If, however, guardians subscribe to a broader ethic, they will see their participation in the community and their advising the community in matters in which they are experts, as a necessary function of their individuality rather than as a supererogatory obligation.

Communities that value their peace and individuals within such communities must only glance at history to realize the pragmatic, aside from the moral, value of beneficence. If healers no longer look after the good of those to be healed, guardians no longer are interested in the good of those whom they are appointed to protect and communities no longer care for the welfare of their members, ethics becomes a cold and peculiar concept. As things stand today, entrepreneurialism and crass individualism have produced a dangerous state of affairs. The times are ripe for the pendulum to swing back, for the community to realize its obligation towards all members, and for the individuals in the community to acknowledge that their neighbor's welfare is, indeed, their legitimate concern. They may do so on theoretical grounds (the theory of the minimalist ethic is ontologically flawed), on practical grounds (no one thinks of community in a purely minimal fashion and communities so constituted cannot and, in fact, do not endure) or on purely humanitarian grounds (allowing some to suffer while others enjoy opulent luxuries affronts one's sense of what human dignity is about): if we as thinking, feeling, and suffering humans wish to have solidarity and peace, caring for our neighbor and meeting his/her basic needs becomes a necessity and participating in building a compassionate community which ensures our neighbor's welfare becomes our individual obligation.[29]

REFERENCES

1. Toulmin, S. (1981). The tyranny of principle. *Hastings Center Report, 11*(4): 31-39.

2. Churchill, L.R., Siman J.J. (1986) Principles and the search for moral certainty. *Social Science and Medicine, 23*: 461-468.

3. Gough, W. (1957). *The social contract.* New York: Oxford University Press;

4. Laslett, P. (1972). Social contract. In P. Edwards (Ed.) *The encyclopedia of philosophy.* New York: Macmillan.

5. Levin, M. (1973). Social contract. In P.P. Weiner (Ed.) *Dictionary of the history of ideas, 4*, New York: Charles Scribner's Sons.

6. Loewy, E.H. (1989). *A textbook of medical ethics.* New York: Plenum Publishers.

7. Hobbes, T. (1962). *Leviathan.* New York: Collier.

8. Locke, J. (1980). In C.E. Macpherson (Ed.) *Second treatise of government.* Indianapolis, IN: Hackett Publishing Co.

9. Rousseau, J.J. (1972). In R. Grimsley (Ed.) *Du Contrat Social.* Oxford: Oxford University Press.

10. Loewy, E.H. (1989). Communities, entrepreneurialism and health care. In *The clinical relationship: Towards a hermeneutical perspective.* Indianapolis, IN: University of Indiana Press.

11. Loewy, E.H. (1988). Commodities, needs and health care: A community perspective. In U.J. Jensen & E.D. Mooney forthcoming book.

12. Loewy, E.H. (1988). Communities, self-causation and the natural lottery. *Social Science and Medicine, 26*, 1133-1139.

13. Nozick, R. (1974). *Anarchy, state and utopia.* New York: Basic Books.

14. Engelhardt, H.T. (1986). *The foundations of bioethics.* New York: Oxford University Press.

15. Niebuhr, R. (1957). Rationing and democracy. In D.R. Robertson (Ed.) *Love and justice.* Philadelphia: Westminster Press.

16. Loewy, E.H. (1987). Not by reason alone: A review of H. Tristram Engelhardt's *Foundations of bioethics. Journal of Medical Humanities and Bioethics*, *8* (1), 67-72.

17. Loewy, E.H. (1988). AIDS and the human community. *Social Science and Medicine*, *27*(4), 297-303.

18. Pellegrino, E.D. & Thomasma, D.C. (1988). *For the patient's good: The restoration of beneficence to health care.* New York: Oxford University Press.

19. Zuckerman, M.B. (1989, July). Dreams, Myth and Reality. *U.S. News and World Report*, *25*, p. 68.

20. Gold, A.R. (1989, July). The struggle to make do without health insurance. *New York Times*, *30*, p. 1.

21. Engelhardt, H.T. (1988). Morality for the medical-industrial complex: A code of ethics for the mass marketing of health care. *New England Journal of Medicine*, *319* (16), 1086-1089.

22. Loewy, E.H. (in press). Medizinische ethik im schatten der Amerikanisierung des gesundheitswesens. *Berliner Arzteblatt.*

23. Loewy, E.H. (1989). Communities, entrepreneurialism and health care. In D. Schultz & W. Sherlock (Eds.) *The clinical relationship: Towards a hermeneutical perspective.* Indianapolis, IN: University of Indiana Press.

24. Loewy, E.H. (in press). Commodities, needs and health care. In. U.J. Jensen and G. Mooney (Eds.) *Changing values in medicine and health care decision making.* New York: Wiley and Sons.

25. Morison, R.S. (1984). The limits of autonomy. *Hastings Center Report*, *14*(6), 43-49.

26. Cassell, E. (1977). The function of medicine. *Hastings Center Report*, 7(6), 16-19.

27. Bassford, H.A. (1982). The justification of medical paternalism. *Social Science and Medicine*, *16*, 731-739.

28. Loewy, E.H. (1987). Treatment decisions in the mentally impaired: Limiting but not abandoning treatment. *New England Journal Of Medicine*, *317*, 1465-1469.

29. Loewy, E.H. (1989). Suffering, moral worth and medical ethics: A new beginning. *Bridges*, *1*(3/4), 107-141.

Managing Guardianships of the Elderly: Protection and Advocacy as Public Policy

Lloyd Hull, MPA, JD
Gary E. Holmes, MLS, MS
Ronald H. Karst, PhD

SUMMARY. Guardianships and conservatorships are currently used to carry out public policy concerning protection of and advocacy for elderly people who cannot care for themselves. This article analyzes this public policy with the idea in mind that the legal aspects of guardianships and conservatorships must be linked with clinical assessment in order for public agencies to provide high quality, need-based services for individual clients. The article also explores the notion that case management for such clients involves coordination of services between the court system and human services providers.

Guardianships and conservatorships are the methods our society uses to protect older people who lack the capacity to protect themselves. By the year 2000, there will be 5.1 million Americans over the age of 85 (Genskow, 1988). Many of these people will become disabled physically, mentally, or both. Courts around the country will appoint guardians or conservators for many of these people so that medical and human services can be monitored by a designated person to safeguard the welfare of an incapacitated person.

Lloyd Hull is an attorney with the Social and Rehabilitation Services of Kansas, Docking State Office Building, Topeka, KS 66612. Gary E. Holmes is also employed by the Social and Rehabilitation Services of Kansas, and is a doctoral student at the School of Social Work, University of Kansas, Topeka. Ronald H. Karst is Associate Professor of Rehabilitation Services Education in the Division of Counselor Education and Rehabilitation Programs at Emporia State University, 1200 Commerical, Emporia, KS 66801.

A court's action in appointing a guardian or a conservator is aimed in part at *stabilization* of services to sustain some quality of life and a sense of well-being. The court's action represents the beginning of "official" advocacy through a responsible person to monitor services and to oversee personal matters. Incompetency hearings allow the courts to consider the extent of physical or mental disabilities and to evaluate community resources to meet the client's needs (Peters, Schmidt, & Miller, 1985). The courts establish a communication link among the legal system, human service providers, and the medical care providers to enhance the public policy of protection.

This paper explores this relationship between the legal and human service communities and focuses upon the role client assessment and professional case management play in ensuring that the public policy is carried out. Finally, the paper offers suggestions to help human service providers respond to the needs of the courts and the clients alike. The courts' perspective is a legal one and not a clinical one. The courts and the guardian or conservator must rely upon the clinical assessment done by human service providers or other helpers to determine actual client needs. This joint effort to fulfill the public policy of protection and of meeting client needs is reflected in the ways in which the two arenas, legal and clinical, interact synergistically. Whereas the courts seek stabilization of care and well-being through the standards imposed by law, service providers rely upon their own professional standards and ethics to assess needs and to provide care. The need for standardized gerontological assessment methods has been recognized (Scogin & Perry, 1986) and may represent an attempt by the service community to match the courts' aim of stabilization of care through higher standards for evidence. The ideal meeting of court and clinician would match standardized laws with standardized assessment, thereby giving the client and the public a higher quality of protection.

THE LAW AND PUBLIC POLICY

Guardianships can be used to provide high quality, powerful intervention into the lives of elderly who have been abused and exploited. That power can be quickly corrupted or perverted and can have a devastating effect upon the often helpless population this intervention was meant to help. The law as a tool to mold and shape society can develop positive programs and legislation to encourage self reliance and independence of the elderly or it can foster dependence.

The public policymaker must strike a balance between legislation that provides legitimate safeguards to protect the elderly from others and the need to protect the constitutional liberties of the most fragile. The disabled individual does not willingly forfeit his or her rights but may be unable to safeguard them. It is the responsibility of those in the legal community and human services to ensure that all those disabled in our society have the same rights as any other group.

The concept of a guardian is a long-held legal tradition. Ancient kings were seen as the "protector" of their peoples and kingdoms under the concept of *parens patriae*. Similarly, children and the so-called feeble-minded have long been seen as in need of protection (Blackstone, 1889). The focus of modern statutory and case law has led away from the mere labeling of an individual to a determination of his or her decision-making capability.

The court must find the proposed ward to be a disabled or incapacitated person under legal terminology before a guardianship can be imposed. The Unified Probate Code (UPC 5-101(1)) states "'incapacitated person' means any person who is impaired by reason of mental illness, mental deficiency, physical illness or disability, advanced age, chronic use of drugs, chronic intoxication or other cause (except minority) to the extent that he lacks sufficient understanding or capacity to make or communicate responsible decisions concerning his person." The above definition is now used to some degree in most state statutes; the wording may present problems because such a broad criterion may be used in an arbitrary manner.

A guardianship can be held in conjunction with a conservatorship or separately. The establishment of a guardianship in most jurisdictions provides for the personal needs of the proposed ward, including health care, personal safety, shelter, food, clothing, and education. This does not mean that the guardian must provide those things personally, but he or she must see that they are provided to the ward. The conservatorship, on the other hand, must contend with the administration of real and personal property, and other benefits. Both the guardian and conservator must safeguard against exploitation.

A guardianship or conservatorship may be full or plenary, encompassing all matters of an individuals's life or "limited." A limited guardianship allows the court to match protection with the appropriate level of need for each individual. A plenary guardianship may create loss of most constitutional rights, including the right to make contracts, to vote, and to drive a car. It may also result in the loss of the right to make judgments about medical or psychological care. This can mean that an individual may not have input into medical surgery or psychiatric hospitalization and may lose the right to control personal property. An adjudication of disability under the criteria of "clear and convincing evidence" must be determined by a judge or jury.

Following the filing of a petition, a preliminary order will be issued by the court naming time and place of hearing and appointing counsel (called guardian ad litem in some states) to represent the proposed ward. The proposed ward usually has the right to independent counsel. However, because most elderly persons and others who have petitions filed against them are indigent and have no active family participation, there is seldom any opportunity to examine this right. The order of the court may also mandate some evaluation by a specific physician or clinician.

The elderly who must attend such hearings, in many instances, have not been involved in legal proceedings and cannot understand legal documents or their ramifications. When an elderly person has no friends or family for emotional support, he or she must face an unfamiliar and often unfriendly environment alone. Frequently, the assigned counsel has neither the time nor the desire to become involved in a "probate" case. Such a situation can create a nightmare world for the elderly person who might already have medical or emotional problems. He or she may be frightened and left to drift in a disinterested judicial system.

In most states a hearing to determine legal disability is held before a district or magistrate judge. In some states the court may have hearings in alternative settings which are more convenient for the proposed ward, such as a nursing home or a hospital. Frequently, such a hearing will result from testimony of a physician indicating that attendance by the proposed ward at a court hearing may endanger the physical and mental condition of the individual. About half of the states allow for a jury trial in a guardianship hearing, normally heard before a six person jury. In practice very few guardianship petitions result in jury trials because the informality allowed in guardianships hearings provides for an easy acceptance of the petition. Because many proposed wards are indigent or have limited financial resources, few appointed attorneys are willing to invest the time that a jury trial would demand.

Recent research indicates that in many courts guardianships are far too easy to obtain. An Associated Press study of guardianships revealed that in a large percentage of cases neither the proposed ward nor his or her appointed or obtained counsel was present at the guardianship hearing. The same study revealed that fifteen states do not require counsel for a proposed ward and twenty-six states do not grant the right to a jury trial in a guardianship hearing (cited in Subcommittee on Health and Long Term Care of the Select Committee on Aging, 1987). Guardianship hearings have been criticized for lack of notice to the proposed ward and other appropriate persons and for relaxed rules of evidence at the adjudication (Subcommittee on Housing & Consumer Interests of the Select Committee on Aging, 1988).

Frequently, a physician's statement may be accepted by the court without other testimony. Such statements may be brief and accepted blindly by the counsel of the proposed ward and the court. A physician may fail to understand the difference between disorientation due to physical or emotional problems and symptoms such as those that result from Alzheimer's Disease (Iris, 1988). Physicians may see patients for short periods and may work from the same bias and stereotyping of the elderly as do other medically-oriented professions in their analyses of patient diagnoses. The fact that the proposed ward's physician may be biased about the elderly should not be surprising. However, this lack of objectivity means a great deal to the patients who have trusted their physicians to safeguard their interests (Goodenough, 1988). Such an experience can cause an elderly patient to lose trust in his or her personal physician, in institutions, in his or her attorney, and in the court.

The problem of bias in a physician's statement may be magnified by the desires of the proposed ward's family or another interested party, such as a social worker. When the proposed ward's family supports a guardianship, the likelihood that the petition will be successful is almost guaranteed. The proposed ward may be unwilling or incapable of resisting the support of the guardianship petition. Frequently, communication problems caused by disease, emotional stress or inability to hear, result in an elderly person appearing incompetent or disabled. Medications can also affect the ability of an elderly person to communicate and to participate in guardianship proceedings (Goodenough).

In virtually all jurisdictions, no objective standards exist for the measure of mental capacity by a physician in the preparation of a medical statement for a guardianship hearing. This seems peculiar when compared with the other evaluations a physician may prepare, since all are based upon a standardized criteria (Goodenough). Standardized criteria for guardianship set by statute might prevent a lack of objectivity toward elders.

Attorneys, like physicians, suffer from the same bias and stereotyping that characterize the rest of society in it's approach to the elderly. Most attorneys tend to avoid indigent clients, especially indigent elderly persons who may be disabled. The attorneys who do help such people are usually appointed by the court or they are involved in a legal aid organization. Most lawyers do not know how to deal with elderly or other disabled persons who cannot communicate clearly or logically. Attorneys tend to want to get such cases over quickly. The clients are not likely to complain or to sue for malpractice. Like the physician, the attorney often has no source of information about the client other than the proposed ward's family or social worker. They often accept the medical statement of the physician without question and defer to the judgment of the physician. In most cases, the physician is not called upon to testify in court, but the medical statement is entered into the case file.

Attorneys should be urged to look beneath the surface in their dealings with the elderly and should be cautioned against acting upon the belief that physical disability is indicative of a mental condition. There is no evidence that the elderly suffer to any degree from loss of intelligence nor do they have a greater degree of psychological or emotional problems than do other ages of the population (Smith, 1988). While our society has come a long way in providing self-determination and due process to individuals with mental incapacity, when the elderly are brought into the legal system, a different standard seems to apply. The elderly are somehow handled with imprecise procedures and obsolete legislation (Rosoff & Gottlieb, 1987).

An attorney or guardian ad litem must represent his or her client as a "zealous advocate." However, there is some question as to whether an attorney should attempt to avoid the appointment of a guardian if the client is disabled or if that attorney should advance the "best interests" of his or her client before the court. The trend presently appears to be moving toward the role of the attorney as an "adversarial advocate" for the client (Frolik, 1987). By viewing the guardianship hearing as an adversarial arena, the counsel for a proposed ward can do much to advance procedural safeguards and to protect the constitutional rights of his or her client. The informality of guardianship hearings has encouraged attorneys to underestimate the serious proposition underlying a guardianship petition. Attorneys or guardians ad litem appointed in such cases have tended to have no specific guidelines for their own behavior in guardianship cases.

Courts are beginning to distinguish the concept of *substituted judgment* from that of *best interests*. The counsel or guardian ad litem may be called upon by the court to follow the letter of the law if no pre-disability preferences were expressed by the client (Pollard, 1987). Many attorneys may find this concept of best interest to be more compatible with the traditional legal ethics which make the client's welfare the primary goal. This distinction may signal a trend away from the guardian ad litem method and toward client advocacy and a more adversarial role for attorneys.

States may be moving toward a standardization of requirements for attorneys or guardians ad litem who act as counsel in guardianship cases. Such measures may increase and safeguard rights and ensure that a thorough investigation is conducted in each case (Morrissey, 1982). Mandated conduct would ensure that any hearings are held in an adversarial framework to protect the rights of the proposed ward and safeguard his or her constitutional freedoms.

A recent study indicated that guardianship cases are rarely monitored properly by the court or advocacy groups. The study found that 82% of cases sampled did not have complete records of accounting for financial records and contact with the ward. Courts also frequently failed to impose sanctions against guardians even when problems were found. Few wards were ever given restoration of capacity (Peters, Schmidt & Miller). However, as with all public policy problems, this one is not so easily solved; courts are already burdened with cases. Perhaps the best public policy solution would be to file fewer guardianships and seek alternatives within communities for the needs of the elderly.

Many profoundly mentally retarded individuals housed in state facilities must have guardians to safeguard their interests and to prevent abuse at the hands of caregivers. For these individuals it is important that the system work properly to monitor both the care given by the facilities and the care given by the guardian in providing for his or her ward's interests. Guardianships can often be important legal tools to prevent similar abuse or neglect of elderly persons and, as long as proper constitutional safeguards are provided, they can be appropriate tools for advocates.

However, there are also other avenues to provide protection of the elderly who are at risk. More states are now implementing a medical durable power of attorney for the elderly and other disabled individuals. These are legal documents authorizing others to make medical decisions and continue in the event of disability. The most important criterion in a medical power of attorney is that the person (elderly or otherwise) must not be legally disabled at the time of the signing of the document. The individual contemplating the time when he or she might be disabled has the right to determine who will act on his or her behalf to make important decisions. Kansas, for example, implemented a medical durable power of attorney in July, 1989, to join a handful of other states that have such statutes. The use of limited guardianships would also be an effective tool to safeguard the rights of the proposed ward.

CLINICAL ISSUES

The guardianship process has been criticized for sanctioning the loss of autonomy for the elderly by viewing such loss as the logical outcome of providing legal protection (Iris). This criticism, however, may have as much to do with the quality of assessment conducted by human service providers as it does with any shortcoming on the courts' part. A court is not a clinical entity and may not have adequate information to distinguish good assessments from bad. It may not be able to recognize the degree of autonomy of which an individual is capable unless that capability is carefully explained by clinicians presenting an assessment to the court. Because personal and environmental characteristics interact to determine an individual's degree of independence (Mathews & Seekins, 1987), the potential for autonomy is dependent upon the quality of the clinician's assessment of the client's characteristics *as presented* to the court.

A clinical failure in this process brings up other issues of how our society views the elderly. We have official public policies to protect the elderly but we may also harbor the erroneous belief that the elderly deserve a different brand of human services, one which focuses on minimum or maintenance care. Health care providers may lack the willingness and expertise to deal with older people with disabilities while other care providers may believe that the elderly are only entitled to "maintenance" services as a token gesture against physical and mental decline and death (Myers, 1985).

Dependency itself is not appropriate clinical evidence of the need for a guardian or conservator, although it may be a legal criterion. One of the important roles that assessment plays in helping the legal system carry out the public policy of protection of the elderly is that of providing accurate information so the courts can make sound decisions. Assessing needs and levels of independence of the elderly should encourage maximum functioning (Finnerty-Fried, 1985). If a person's level of mental or physical functioning translates into the need for a guardian or conservator, the court should be helped to understand the clinical implications of this fact within the context of standardized assessment methods.

Six areas of holistic assessment for physical disability proposed

(Mathews and Seekins) to unite the rehabilitation perspective with that found in many independent living centers include the following:

- Physical ability
- Knowledge and skills
- Values and goals
- Physical environment
- Social environment
- Systemic variables

If pertinent information about psychosocial and intellectual functioning were added, the list would represent the major areas of a client's life. Clinical assessment can describe capacities and incapacities in terms of everyday living from the perspective of gerontology. The court can use this assessment to decide whether to appoint a guardian or conservator and how much control he or she should assume. An assessment can also help the guardian ad litem take a proactive advocacy posture by asking the court to limit the control of the guardian or conservator only to those areas in which the need is clearly defined by objective data. In a legal sense, the guardian ad litem may remain neutral by investigating the facts of the case on behalf of the court (Riess-Curtis, 1989). This does not mean the guardian ad litem limits his or her activities to legal motions. The "facts" of the case that establish competency or incompetency are the same sort the clinician can provide in a comprehensive assessment. The guardian ad litem wants to discover the facts that point to the need for protection and to the limits of that need.

Guardians are often appointed on the basis of conclusionary psychiatric diagnoses instead of on the basis of the client's functional capacities to behave in competent ways (Scogin & Perry). The comprehensive functional assessment can give the court some alternative to total guardianship as it attempts to fulfill the public policy of protection. An important clinical issue in this regard is that functional assessments that address all aspects of life may also point to the very things from which the elderly client needs protection. Older persons who are incapacitated by physical or mental disabilities may be at a greater risk from others (Pillemer & Finkelhor,

1988). Families may practice physical or psychological abuse or neglect. The guardianship or conservatorship hearing serves as the forum in which these facts may be brought out so the elderly client's case can be fairly adjudicated.

Unfortunately, guardians themselves may present a potential source of elder abuse. For example, a family member appointed as a guardian may use the position as a way of controlling ("getting") the financial resources of the incapacitated elderly person. In such instances, it is possible that the family member may be in direct conflict with the advocacy role of the guardian ad litem. This conflict can involve clinicians if they are called upon by the court or guardian ad litem to prepare a functional assessment to determine the client's ability to handle financial matters. As a more drastic example, a family member appointed guardian may become involved in an adversarial relationship with a guardian ad litem over whether the life of the client is to be prolonged by artificial life support (Kart, 1981). In such a situation, *abuse* versus *caring* may become an uncertain concept for all those involved, including the court.

An important point to be made here is that the client can be the best source of information about his or her own functional capacities. The clinician assessing needs can discuss with those clients who can do so how they perceive their own needs. Clinicians who have experience with gerontological issues will understand that a client can remain independent and still have some problems with self-care. Such a clinician is less likely to equate partial dependency with total incapacitation. The clinician acts as a client advocate by exploring areas of strength and need so that protection may be designed to suit individual situations.

A need assessment cannot be separated in any meaningful way from a care or treatment plan based upon that assessment. If the court is to entertain the notion of *degree* of independence and capacity, it must also view the client as a dynamic, changing human being. The court has need to understand an estimate of *current* functioning and of *future* functioning as the care or treatment plan unfolds. Again, the court depends on human service providers or health care providers to present a summary of the immediate situation, prognosis, care or treatment recommendations, and probable outcomes. A holistic gerontological assessment not only helps the service provider contribute as an advocate to ensure the well being of the individual, it helps providers avoid the "maintenance services only" mentality which the courts have accepted as evidence so often in the past to the detriment of many incapacitated elderly persons.

PLANNING HUMAN SERVICES

People with disabilities in other age groups are living longer and are experiencing many of the chronic health problems usually associated with older age (Batavia, De Jong, Halstead, & Smith, 1989). Assessing and planning care for people with multiple disabilities is even more difficult. A comprehensive need-based assessment tied closely to a care and treatment plan helps the courts understand how different disabilities may exacerbate legal incompetencies. As assessment becomes more complex so, too, does the care plan emerging from the assessment.

The logical sequence beginning with a comprehensive assessment, through service planning, to providing services, must contain a recognizable provision for decision-making. The court, the guardian, the guardian ad litem, the case manager or assessor, the family, and the client, to whatever degree possible, must understand both process and content of the care plan. All must also understand how future decisions are to be made, who will make them, and who will carry them out.

Medical evidence may be a relatively brief summary of the facts as seen from the medical perspective. Case managers and evaluators who have more indepth knowledge of gerontological issues may present a better "picture" of the client's needs and options. A physician may present testimony based solely on a medical examination without knowledge of the client's family support system or of the client's lack of such support. Conversely, human services planners may be in a better position to weigh factors of family dysfunction which may contribute to elder abuse. Kosberg (1988) suggested the following family characteristics which represent "high risk" for the elderly:

- Lack of family support
- Caregiver reluctance
- Overcrowding
- Isolation
- Marital conflict
- Economic pressures
- Intra-family problems
- Desire for institutionalization
- Disharmony in shared responsibility

Few physicians would have the expertise, time, or inclination to evaluate family systems. Medical data do not always communicate to the court an appreciation for the specific areas in the client's life in which he or she can retain independence and autonomy. To the degree to which medicine has turned aging into "illness" (Zola, 1978), basic medical information may even confuse the courts and families. A caring family trying to protect an older family member may draw inappropriate conclusions from what a doctor says. The uncaring family may use medical information as an excuse to take independence and autonomy away from the elderly family member by extrapolating a static medical report into a "no hope" condition. Evaluators and case managers who provide functional assessment and supportive services may offer the court its only alternative to this static and hopeless view of the client's future.

Family members who reside great distances from the client and the court may find it "easier" to accept a medical verdict of hopelessness and to accept the "wisdom" of the need only for maintenance services. The mobility which helped alter the traditional form of the extended family may place more burden upon the court to decide competency. That is, the family may leave the decision to the court and not offer supportive care. Feelings of obligation by adult children have declined as society has built new programs for medical and social insurance; the spouse of an elderly person may be unprepared to deal with the responsibilities of care (Aguilera & Messick, 1986).

A family member who has been appointed guardian may take little interest in monitoring services to appraise the client's quality of life. Such perfunctory attendance to the client's welfare may encourage others to provide minimum services or may simply allow services to stagnate at the maintenance level. The guardian ad litem, if appointed, may assist the court in discovering such practices and may call upon case managers to assess level of need in relation to quality of services currently being provided.

The ability to act rationally and to choose for one's own good underlies common sense definitions and legal definitions of mental illness (Moore, 1984). By association, medical evidence may conjure up such definitions in the minds of the courts and families trying to decide on the fate of the elderly. The presence of a medical disability may be taken as "proof" of a client's lack of mental abilities. The court and family may innocently imagine a medical condition to be the equivalent of mental illness, a malady which traditionally relieves the client of both personal responsibility and personal choice. This attitude may also relieve a family of any guilt it might harbor for usurping control over the elderly family member. Human services and supportive care providers should furnish information to the court to prevent such association by clearly defining and limiting the areas in life in which the client has or does not have functional capacity to act in his or her own best interest.

Without comprehensive assessment and care planning, the court may only be able to carry out the public policy of protection to a limited extent. If evidence is limited only to that reflected by a medical report, it is possible for the court, the client's family, the guardian, and the guardian ad litem to become unwitting partners in a policy of "blameless," slow euthanasia. Professional assessment and case management planning can, however, help preclude such an occurrence by giving information that courts have not traditionally had when making decisions about guardianship and conservatorship issues. The impact of this information is that the client gets better "justice" from the courts and better care from available resources identified by the assessor or case manager. The outdated philosophy of maintenance services thus has less chance to affect the quality of the client's life.

Case assessment and management methods appropriate for guardianship or conservatorship issues can provide family members with client information that will help families cope. Adults with aging parents, for example, may experience stress from role changes, care-giving, decision-making, dependency, and death (Myers, 1988), all issues which can be addressed by assessment and case management plans. Whereas the court's main role is to decide on the competency of the client, human service providers conducting needs assessment or planning care can offer family members information on what to do about specific problems related to functional incompetencies. This information may reduce family stress and increase attention to the client's immediate needs.

Elderly people who live in total care environments may deteriorate prematurely (Tomine, 1986). Careful needs assessment and case management can help alter this outcome by minimizing services that are oriented toward custodialism. In guardianship and conservatorship cases the idea of extending the "least invasive" care translates as less protection and as more freedom. The client makes decisions in those areas of life in which he or she possesses functional capacity. By limiting protection, the case manager can help the client retain personal control over part of his or her own life. Autonomy is safeguarded while the client has legal protection in those areas in which he or she lacks capacity. Autonomy and dependence may then go hand in hand; the client can experience freedom from total control imposed by others while enjoying legal protection as needed.

CONCLUSION

Guardianships and conservatorships have been viewed as an outmoded method of protection because they have been established without legal due process and without the "patient" being present during the proceeding (Torrey, 1983). Courts still follow the legal concept of "substituted judgment" when allowing one person to make binding decisions for another (Kart). However, the trend toward the appointment of guardians ad litem and the use of professional needs assessment and case management are giving courts, families, and clients a new method of evaluating the nature of the need for substitution of judgment. These newer sources of information assist the courts in fulfilling the public policy of protection of the elderly by helping them make more informed, objective decisions about how guardianships and conservatorships are to be limited and how those who fill these roles are to behave on the client's behalf.

Guardianships and conservatorships will remain important methods of extending protective laws to those who lack functional competency. The spirit of those laws resides in the idea that the loss of personal control which is given up in favor of protection should be held to a minimum. Courts now can rely on human services professionals for assessments and care plans which reflect the degree of client need. Fewer courts will routinely accept brief medical information as the best evidence. Although medical information will always be important in such cases, courts will increasingly rely upon information which spells out how much protection a client needs.

Clinical assessment, case management, and guardians ad litem can be expensive services. Although their value to the public policy of protection has already been demonstrated in the courts, our society has yet to perfect a sound public policy to ensure that clinical assessment is available to every citizen who needs them. We have not formulated a method whereby the elderly who need partial care can be readily identified at the community level. It is still possible for a family member to be appointed guardian and then to leave the elderly ward to fend for himself of herself. However, the courts are taking the important first steps to improve the way in which protective public policies are carried out.

Public policy of protection can be carried out without undue invasion of the lives and privacy of elderly people. The courts will continue to seek stabilization of services as a way of stabilizing quality of life. When protection is warranted by the severity of incapacity, the courts can evaluate evidence and testimony offered by different disciplines that have knowledge of gerontological issues.

As important as the courts are to fulfilling the public policy of protection for elderly persons, they do not make those policies. Protective laws are written as precisely as possible on behalf of all citizens who may one day need that protection. To give the elderly this protection does not require that a court decide each competency case on an either-or basis. Courts now have access to clinicians to help provide information to support decisions on the basis of degree of need. The relationship which exists between the court and the clinician helps protect the individual client from too much or too little official protection. When viewed as a partnership relationship, the interaction between court and clinician helps give the elderly access to those human services that can help sustain quality and dignity of life.

REFERENCES

Aguilera, D.C. & Messick, J.M. (1986). *Crisis intervention: Theory and methodology* (5th ed.). St. Louis: C.V. Mosby.

Batavia, A.I., De Jong, G., Halstead, L.S., & Smith, Q.W. (1989). Primary medical services for people with disabilities. *American Rehabilitation*, Winter 1988-1989, 9-12 and 26-27.

Blackstone, I.W. (1989). *Commentaries*, 304, 460.

Finnerty-Fried, P. (1985). Adapting rehabilitation counseling for older persons. *Rehabilitation Counseling Bulletin*, *29*, 135-142.

Frolik, L.A. (1981). Plenary guardianship. *Arizona Law Review*, *23*, 600-660.

Genskow, J.K. (1988). Independent living programs and services for older persons with disabilities. *Journal of Rehabilitation*, *54* (4), 43-47.

Goodenough, G.K. (1988). The lack of objectivity of physician evaluations in geriatric guardianship cases. *Journal of Contemporary Law*, *14*, 53-59.

Iris, M.A. (1988). Guardianship and the elderly: A multi-perspective view of the decisionmaking process. *The Gerontologist*, *28* (Supplement), 39-45.

Kart, C.S. (1981). In the matter of Earle Spring: Some thoughts on one court's approach to senility. *The Gerontologist*, *21*, 417-423.

Kosberg, J.I. (1988). Preventing elder abuse: Identification of high risk factors prior to placement decisions. *The Gerontologist*, *28*, 43-50.

Mathews, R.M. & Seekins, T. (1987). An interactional model of independence. *Rehabilitation Psychology*, *32*, 165-172.

Moore, M.S. (1984). *Law and psychiatry: Rethinking the relationship*. New York: Cambridge University Press.

Morrissey, M. (1982). Guardian ad litem: An educational program in Virginia. *The Gerontologist*, *22*, 301-304.

Myers, J.E. (1985). Using links to help older persons with transitions. *Rehabilitation Counseling Bulletin*, *29*, 143-149.

Myers, J.E. (1988). The mid/late life generation gap: Adult children with aging parents. *Journal of Counseling and Development*, *66*, 331-335.

Peters, R., Schmidt, W.C., Jr., & Miller, K.S. (1985). Guardianship of the elderly in Tallahassee, Florida. *The Gerontologist*, *25*, 532-539.

Pillemer, K. & Finkelhor, D. (1988). The prevalence of elder abuse: A random sample survey. *The Gerontologist*, *28*, 51-57.

Pollard, C.T. (1987). *Rasmussen vs. Fleming*. *Issues in Law and Medicine*, *3*, 297-310.

Riess-Curtis, C. (1989). A clinical-legal perspective, a comfortable accommodation. *New England Journal of Human Services, 9* (2), pp. 11-12.

Rosoff, A.J. & Gottlieb, G.L. (1987). Preserving personal autonomy for the elderly – competency, guardianship and Alzheimer's disease. *The Journal of Legal Medicine*, *8*, (1), 1-47.

Scogin, F. & Perry, J. (1986). Guardianship proceedings with older adults: The role of functional assessment and gerontologists. *Law and Psychology Review*, *10*, 123-128.

Smith, L.F. (1988). Representing the elderly client and addressing the question of competence. *Journal of Contemporary Law*, *14*, 61-95.

Subcommittee on Health and Long Term Care of the House Select Committee on Aging (1987). Abuses in guardianship of the elderly and infirm: A national disgrace. A report by the Chairman, 100th U.S. Congress, 1st Session.

Subcommittee on Housing and Consumer Interests of the Select Committee on Aging (1988). Surrogate decision making for adults: Model standards to ensure quality guardianship and representative payeeship services. A report by the Chairman, 100th U.S. Congress, 2nd Session.

Tomine, S. (1986). Private practice in gerontological counseling. *Journal of Counseling and Development*, *64*, 406-409.

Torrey, E.F. (1983). *Surviving schizophrenia: A family manual.* New York: Harper & Row.

Unified Probate Code (UPC 5-101 < 1 >).

Zola, I.K. (1978). Medicine as an institution of social control. In D. Tuckett & J.M. Kaufert (Eds.), *Basic Readings in Medical Sociology*. pp. 254-260.

Avoiding Guardianship

George J. Alexander, JD, LLM, JSD

SUMMARY. The lack of progress in guardianship reform during the last thirty years is described, and some of the current efforts to improve the system are discussed. The use of the living will and durable power of attorney is proposed as a more promising approach to elder autonomy than working within the present guardianship system. In spite of differences among the states and restrictions that limit the utility of the living will, it holds out more promise than guardianship as a legal tool of general application.

Asserted to be compassionate, guardianship[1] can be (and most often is) a frightening, debilitating, and insensitive imposition of state authority on citizens making decisions about their private lives. Its effects, both financial and psychological, are often horrendous. I would like to review the lack of progress in this field during the last thirty years and to discuss an alternative approach which I find more helpful.

I am a long term opponent of guardianship. Numerous case studies of abuse can be found in my prior writings (Alexander and Lewen, 1972; Alexander, 1988; Alexander, 1979). Without reviewing them, a single report reflects one of the main reasons for much of my complaints. The Benjamin Rose Institute undertook an illuminating study of protective services some years ago. Unlike prior studies, which merely asked about the quality of assistance, it added an additional question: How much did protective services increase longevity? The results were startling. Those "protected"

George J. Alexander is Professor of Law and former Dean of Santa Clara University School of Law.

This article is adapted from the author's keynote address to the Second National Guardianship Association Conference in Chicago, IL on October 31, 1988.

died in greater proportions than a control group in the first year and continued to do so in succeeding years (Benjamin Rose Institute, 1974).

Nor should it be difficult to understand the mortality findings. Losing control of the right to make their own decisions concerning health care and losing the right to spend their own money as they choose are devastating for most people. Add to that the prospect of being placed in a nursing home or, worse yet, a mental institution and you can imagine the distress facing the protected ward.

As the studies I shall now discuss make clear, guardianship is disproportionately a problem of the elderly. There are, of course, wards in their younger years but most wards are elders. In speaking with groups of elders, I always find great agreement that retaining control of their lives is an important priority. Supporters of guardianships, forced institutionalization, and other forms of surrogate management certainly exist but I am not one of them. And neither are the elder audiences.

To put things into some perspective, consider three studies of conservatorship, guardianship or its equivalent. The first is a study which a group I directed conducted in upstate New York for the decade 1960-1970 (Alexander and Lewen, 1974). A few of its conclusions may be helpful. Undoubtedly the most depressing was the conclusion reached after examination of the files of all cases: "[I]n almost every case examined the aged incompetent was in a worse position after he was adjudicated incompetent than before." The cases typically appeared to be vehicles for satisfying needs of others, especially the need of the state to be paid for protective services. "No cases were found where the court on the motion of the guardian ad litem or 'friend' of the incompetent or on its own motion took judicial action in order to protect some specific interest of the incompetent. Occasionally the court would act to protect the assets of the estate, but ordinarily it was concerned only with the extent of the legitimate interest of the committee or some third person. Usually the court reviewed the financial transactions of the committee only because some other person who had a residual . . . interest in the estate made some complaint about the management."

As the study used the files of adjudicated incompetents, there is no direct data on the success of defense against guardianship. One measure of probable success can be derived from the data on representation. "The incompetent is frequently not brought to court and his interests are protected through the appointment of a guardian ad litem. Only 16.4% of the New York incompetents, however, had guardians ad litem appearing for them at the hearing." "[T]he only person to take an active role in the decision making process—the incompetency proceeding—are the petitioner and his lawyer."

Equally depressing facts emerged from an empirical study done by the National Senior Citizens Law Center of files in Los Angeles. It focused more directly on the process of declaring persons incompetent. In the 1010 files included in that study, a physician appeared in court in only one case to testify to the condition of the proposed ward. Excepting the 12.2% of cases which were self initiated, 80.1% of the proposed wards were over 60 years old. Only 4.4% of the petitions were dismissed for reasons other than death or disappearance. Only 7.8% of the proposed wards were in court for their hearings and only 2.9% of them were represented by counsel (Horstman, 1975).

To remedy the conditions in California, a group worked on a revision of conservatorship laws. I had the dubious honor of carrying the result to the legislature. The law was strengthened to make the standard for conservatorship more functional. The right of the proposed ward to be represented and to be in court was reiterated in stronger language. Psychological excuses for excluding him or her were expressly rejected as such excuses had routinely been used to keep them out of court. Finally, the law provided that a court investigator would be sent to interview any person still not in court and would report back to the judge (see Alexander, 1977).

Recently, Professor Friedman has produced what can be read as an evaluation of our California reform efforts (Friedman and Savage, 1988). His paper reports on a study of a sample of 214 probate guardianships created between 1982 and 1986 (guardianships which include the power to place a person in a locked facility are created in different proceedings in California. See Cal. Welf. & Inst. Code 5225-5331 (Supp. 1989). Eighty four percent of the guardianships were for people over 60. Only 22.88% of the wards were in attendance at their hearings. Sixty eight percent were adjudged unable to attend. (The sample included 153 files in which the petition was not withdrawn before adjudication). Of these cases, only one was denied, and it was denied for lack of jurisdiction!

Shortly after the Friedman study, the Associated Press published an unprecedented national study of guardianship. It reviewed 70 California guardianship cases and found that 19 (27%) of the wards attended the hearings while ten (14%) were represented by attorneys (Gartes and Castaneda, 1987.) The national data from 2200 cases indicated only 44% were not represented by attorneys and only about half were not present at their hearings. In light of the New York and California experience, those conclusions seem suspect. In the national data, one in 4 had no hearing and in places such as Charlottesville, N.C. or Cleveland, AP reports that a court clerk hears the evidence and issues the order. According to AP 44% of the lawyers were also decision makers in the process.

Of course, procedures are sometimes worse. Associated Press reported that in one of the many states that do not require more than medical certification, one person was given guardianship because the doctor scrawled a note which read "she is incompetent (*sic*) in signing or managing her check." Baltimore courts use an expedited procedure under which hospitals file as guardians then move wards to nursing homes before the petition is approved.

Obviously, if the Friedman study and Associated Press report are a report card of success in changing the effect of the law, reform gets failing grades. What went wrong? Over the course of the years in which I have considered that question, I have persuaded myself that a large part of the problem lies in the fact that the system is essentially not reformable.

A case I brought into court shortly after the new law went into effect is an example of one reason why reform does not work. The judge, accustomed to prior practice, distorted the new provisions in application until they were indistinguishable from the ones they replaced. After all, conservatorship was designed to be of benefit to the ward wasn't it? (Conservatorship of Blatties, 1978).

The other, far more serious, reason reform does not work is that attorneys are seduced in the same manner. The contrast between guardianship representation and criminal defense is amazing. All the more so as it often involves the same attorneys. Consider. When was the last time you heard a criminal defense lawyer brag that she or he facilitated the conviction of her/his client because she or he was persuaded that some time in prison would rehabilitate the client? I assure you, it is often quite possible to make a case that imprisonment is in a client's best interest as perceived by others. Nonetheless, the system will not tolerate a defense lawyer's joining the prosecution in achieving that end over the protestations of the client. Yet lawyers who are clear about criminal defense will cooperate with others to provide protective services for their clients over the protests of the client because they perceive it to be in the client's best interest.

The law is, of course, written using a contrary premise. Often elaborate provisions call for client representation as well as obligatory hearings and detail other aspects of due process. They can all be circumvented if the lawyers and the judge concur in manipulating the process. Many clients seem too debilitated to make trustworthy decisions, and I concede that there are instances in which the client's condition requires concern. In my own experience, however, I have never found it necessary to represent a position other than one to which my client has expressly agreed. As in the criminal analog, I would wonder what I added to the proceedings if I did—other than an endorsement of the opposing lawyer's position.

Speaking positively, there are a number of changes which might improve the process. Both the American Bar Association Commission on Problems of the Elderly and the University of New Mexico's Institute of Public Law have been grappling with recommendations. They both surveyed expert opinions on the subject. Among the better ideas expressed are:

Standards for guardianship should be strict rather than loose and functional rather than medical. That was certainly our intent in the California redraft though I do not like the compromise which ultimately resulted. Of tests for incompetency which are in common use and which should be eliminated one of the worst is old age. It was the reason given for guardianship in 8% of the AP study cases. Who cares about age if the person is competent and who needs age to prove an inability to function in real life? Another inappropriate standard is physical disability. So long as the mind functions, how can one justify removing decision making? One cannot.

Mental illness and all of its analogs should not be the standard either. There are some who have trouble functioning competently who are not likely to be diagnosed as mentally ill for any other purpose. There are many who, for some purpose, are found to be mentally ill who can manage their day to day lives adequately. Most of all, introducing mental illness as a factor swamps proceedings with professional testimony that may obscure the real question of whether the person can function without a surrogate.

Ideally, some procedure should be devised allowing the court to be informed about the day to day functioning of the potential ward. For example, a Court Investigator, of the type appointed in California, could be charged with visiting him or her and reporting back to the court. Ability to manage, whether by oneself or with the help of friends who will remain available, should be conclusive proof of legal competence sufficient to defeat the petition. If a guardianship is established for health care, that alone should not create a surrogacy for financial management. Neither should suffice for involuntary commitment to a locked institution.

Being in danger of imposition by artful and designing people should be eliminated as a factor for guardianship. There may be some legitimacy in identifying increased gullibility as a characteristic of a loss of ability to function. Even there, more energy expended on prosecuting fraud rather than depriving the defrauded of their liberty seems called for. The artful and designing language, on the other hand, is a perfect tool for avaricious family members to use in getting courts to prefer them over strangers by depriving the potential ward of his or her right to the contrary preference. In some settings, preferring a charity or non-familial friend over children or parents may, if all the facts are known, better illustrate acute competency than the need for surrogacy. For similar reasons, family members should not *automatically* be accepted as surrogates.

That brings up another serious problem. Conflicts of interests should be reduced. At its worst, the system is a semi-blind procedure for preferring petitioner's interests over those of the potential ward. It does not examine the reasons for the petitioner having brought the action and, consequently, assumes that he or she acts in the ward's best interest. The cases based on avarice are only one form of conflict of interest. Institutions which are going to profit from providing services—such as nursing homes—should simply be excluded as petitioners and *certainly as surrogates*. Health care professionals, for the same reason, should not end up in legal control of their patients. In the studies I did in New York, the largest petitioner was the state. It also should be debarred at least from providing approval for its own procedures or acceptance of its benefits by making its own officers the persons who sign for the patient. What to do with family members pursuing their own interests is more complicated. It goes too far to debar family from serving as they often are the closest to the potential ward. Perhaps the best that can be done is to attempt to make judges aware of the importance of questioning the petitioner's interests in the outcome of a guardianship hearing.

Appointments of guardians should be reviewed periodically with the burden of proof of need for their continuation falling on the surrogate. Better still, when possible, the guardianship should be set for a temporary period and then automatically terminated.

While it may be a good idea to conserve property for a person who is likely to survive guardianship, the routine conservation of assets for those in long term surrogacy is likely simply to preserve their property for the use of others after their death. Guardians should be held to strict periodic accounting and courts should assure their adequacy either directly or by appointing a court office to manage the task. At the moment, accountings are often not required and are commonly casually approved by courts when required.

It should be reemphasized that the function of surrogacy is to effectuate the wishes of the ward not the surrogate. It should not be legitimate to impose a best interest standard on a ward (as opposed to effectuating his or her own competent wishes). Which of us would be sanguine about being invariably forced to do what is in our best interest even assuming we would trust someone else to figure out what that would be?

Since we have a societal preference for autonomy over surrogacy, an effort should be made to provide public services which would suffice to make some potential wards competent. For example, a money management agency which might contractually provide those services seems preferable to providing them by guardianship. Fee for service options, generally, seem particularly appropriate.

In any event, given the data from the sixties through the present, I am not optimistic about reform of guardianship law. A decade ago I would have said that there has at least been progress in preventing involuntary mental hospitalization. A wave of due process concerns disgorged long term inmates and kept new commitments to defined short periods (see, e.g., Morse, 1982). Unfortunately, very legitimate concern for the homeless has recently turned into a rehospitalization crusade (Morse, 1982), which will have to be resisted with all available resources. In this facet of protective services, as well, seduction of the advocate by the charms of the best interest standard will be a major problem.

My remarks would be incomplete if I did not note that the record of state mismanagement of guardianships has attracted federal attention. Several bills were introduced in Congress in 1988 to set federal standards for guardianship (i.e., H.R. 5266; H.R. 5275). They constitute another attempt to eradicate the abuses of the past by providing stricter rules and more due process.

I recommend that, if any reforms are adopted, someone replicate the prior studies. I pessimistically predict that she or he will find that most wards were not brought to court when they were declared incompetent and that most did not have an attorney contesting guardianship. If so, even though there are other better measures of failure, I would be prepared to condemn the new "reforms" as another failure. Guardianship should certainly not be imposed on people who can manage their affairs adequately. At least, proposed wards should have an opportunity to have that issue decided by a judge who has had a chance to see them.

Unfortunately, following our general societal attitudes about problem solving, many of the solutions to social problems have been interventionist. Protective services have grown enormously as government replaced the family as principal protector. In fact, the state itself brings many guardianship proceedings against its own poor and powerless.

In search of a more promising approach to elder autonomy, I have for some years been espousing a contractual approach. Instead of a frontal attack on surrogacy, I proposed adapting the estate planner's durable power of attorney to become an instrument for preserving individual autonomy. As I indicated in an article a decade ago (Alexander, 1979), I think that such instruments can eliminate guardianships in most cases. While a valid instrument does not actually bar the appointment of a surrogate, the directives concerning assets should survive surrogacy and, at least, make it difficult for an avaricious relative to succeed in plans of self-aggrandizement. It should also provide an agent to resist the other indignities that attend being declared incompetent.

In general, a durable power of attorney is a document by which people create a power which is binding even when they are incapacitated. It is to be distinguished from a general power of attorney which, by common law, becomes ineffective when one becomes incompetent. Making a durable power transfers an earlier competent decision into the hands of an "attorney-in-fact" (a legal term for this type of agent – he or she need not be a lawyer at all) to apply if and when the maker's competence is no longer accepted. Durable power of attorney statutes exist in all of the states and in the District of Columbia.[2]

The durable power of attorney was traditionally used for financial transactions. The attorney-in-fact can be given power to enter into contracts, sign checks, buy or sell property, or to do whatever the principal would like. The attorney-in-fact could then sign on the ward's behalf. In real estate transactions, the durable power can be recorded at the County Recorder's Office. Then the attorney-in-fact can sign deeds, promissory notes, or whatever she or he has been authorized to do.

Another advance directive that was then being developed dealt with terminal medical care. Directives to physicians to remove life support under specified circumstances are now authorized by Natural Death Acts in most states. They are called living wills, a name I have stolen for second generation living wills which combine both fiscal and health care directives into a single document. I believe the term is more appropriately used for a document that expresses all of one's wishes rather than just the wish to facilitate death.

The second generation living will is an effective tool by which to plan for incapacity. It can grant very broad powers and, in effect, can be used to transfer almost all the legal capacity of the principal to another person, the attorney-in-fact, who will act in his or her place. Its use for fiscal decisions is well established. In addition, it can specify the forms of medical treatment the maker wishes and those whom she or he chooses to administer them. A living will is a powerful tool for preventing forms of unwanted treatment as well. This is especially important because of the controversial methods of treatment that can and have been used on the incompetent and the incapacitated. Specifically, a principal can direct her attorney-in-fact to prevent electroshock treatments from being used if that is his or her wish. She can see that any personal or religious preferences are complied with by instructing her representative to insist on them. Absent making such a document, she has no way to guarantee her preferences once she is determined to be incompetent. A living will retains her control over problems which concern her.

I was delighted when California proposed to adopt a new law to extend the concept of durable powers to health care concerns and worked with the Law Revision Commission in its creation (Alexander, 1979). Actually, I doubt that there is need for a specific health care law since the provisions of law allowing durable powers appear broad enough.

As health care laws were proposed, they engendered political pressure concerning provisions which would allow termination of life support for terminal patients. The issue proved divisive. As a result, most health care durable power laws are filled with restrictions. That is unfortunate in an instrument which should appear attractive to the general public. Much worse is the fact that, to date, most states which have passed laws have devised different forms for use and some of them have insisted that their forms be used exclusively. One exclusive form state is Rhode Island. If other states, for example little Rhode Island's neighbors, follow suit the results could be tragic. I expect that courts will apply local law in interpreting a non-resident's documents which may make health care directives invalid in exclusive form states should an out of state maker be there when she or he is stricken. Of course, even in non-exclusive form states, every restriction provides a reason for invalidating a document whether drafted by a resident or not. Contrast the Spartan simplicity of the Alaska law which has merely added health care as an item which may be included in a traditional durable power (Alaska Statutes §13.26.332, Supp. 1989).

A living will is generally now touted as a means of avoiding guardianships. Actually, it does not precisely do that. Usually, it is still theoretically possible to obtain a conservator for an incompetent person even if that person has executed a living will. On the other hand, it will be far more difficult to persuade a judge that a surrogate is required if the proposed ward is adequately provided for by the document. Also, the provisions of the living will provide proof of the maker's competent wishes respecting his or her property and health care which will be difficult to circumvent. That fact should greatly reduce the temptation to file self serving petitions. To make instruments more effective, I recommend nominating the agent (attorney-in-fact) as the guardian should a guardianship be established. Many states honor such nominations as a general matter. Such an appointment guarantees that there will be no conflict between the two.

There is, of course, a potential dark side to living wills as well. The named agents can be just as unscrupulous as court appointed conservators and court supervision will be lacking. For just such reasons, the California Durable Power for Health Care statute expressly forbids health care and institutional representatives from being witnesses for health care directives. The concern for conflicting interests also manifests itself in the requirement that, in addition, at least one witness not be a relative by blood, marriage or adoption and also not be a person who would take from the estate under the will of the maker (California Civil Code, §2432, Supp. 1989). What makes them far preferable in my judgment is that attorneys-in-fact will have been chosen by the ward rather than by a stranger unfamiliar with the ward. Since there is no guarantee against overreaching in any event, let the person most interested be responsible. At least, the ward will not be governed by the notions of a court appointed surrogate. She or he is not left to the possibly conflicting points of view of members of the family or to the views of the attending physicians. The ward will effectively be governed by the mandates of a trustworthy source: his or her own prior competent self.

Several major problems exist with second generation living wills.

I have already mentioned the problem of state restrictions which threaten a document drafted in another state. I have also mentioned the possibility of the choice of an untrustworthy agent. For many prospective wards, especially the very old, finding a person able and willing to serve is a major hurdle. Society may have to promote a volunteer corps of persons willing to serve. Finally, there remains an enormous educational problem in teaching people the importance of making durable powers and instructing them in how to draft them. Many forms exist and I have written a book to help with drafting problems (Alexander, 1979).

Guardianship is under attack from many fronts. It has proven to be a corrosive concept. I believe it inherently defective because it threatens human freedom but many are still attempting reform. In reviewing the last thirty years of development, I conclude that little has been accomplished. The law now provides for an alternative which can avoid guardianship: the second generation living will. I continue to urge that energy be put into perfecting it and that guardianship be discarded as a legal tool of general application.

NOTES

1. The term guardianship is not universally applied to surrogate management. In California, for example, guardianship exists only for minor children but conservatorship applies to what was once known as guardianship of people who have reached the age of 18. Cal. Probate Code 1500-1605 (Supp. 1989). The change of description was heralded as removing the stigma of the former term. Other states use still different names. In this article, the author uses guardianship as a generic term to embody all of them. Whatever it is called, guardianship has similar impact. A rose by any other name . . .; Shakespeare's point applies as well to more malodorous names.

2. Writing a Living Will appendix at 121-124 lists all laws in effect when the book was published.

REFERENCES

Alaska Statutes.

Alexander, G. & Lewin, T. (1972). *The aged and the need for surrogate management*. Syracuse: Syracuse University Press.

Alexander, G. (1977). On being imposed upon by artful and designing people:

The California experience with the involuntary placement of the aged. *San Diego Law Review, 14*, 1083-1099.

Alexander, G. (1979). Premature probate: A different perspective on guardianship for the elderly, *Stanford Law Review, 31*, 1003-1033.

Alexander, G. (1988). *Writing a living will: Using a durable power of attorney.* New York: Praeger Press.

Benjamin Rose Institute. (1974). *Final report: Protective services for older people.* New York.

Benjamin Rose Institute. (1974). *Protective services for older people: Findings from the Benjamin Rose Institute study.* New York.

California Civil Code.

Conservatorship of Blatteis, Superior Court, San Mateo County 1978 (unreported).

Friedman, L. & Savage, A. (1988). Taking care: The law of conservatorship in California, *University of Southern California Law Review, 61*, 273.

Gartes, G. & Castaneda, L. (Sept 20-24, 1987). Guardians of the elderly: A failing system. *San Jose Mercury News*, p.1.

Horstman, P. (1975). Protective services for the elderly: The limits of Parens Patriae, *Missouri Law Review, 40*, 215.

Morse, S. J. (1982). A Preference for liberty: The case against involuntary commitment of the mentally disordered. *California Law Review, 70*, 54-92.

For Product Safety Concerns and Information please contact our EU representative GPSR@taylorandfrancis.com
Taylor & Francis Verlag GmbH, Kaufingerstraße 24, 80331 München, Germany

www.ingramcontent.com/pod-product-compliance
Ingram Content Group UK Ltd.
Pitfield, Milton Keynes, MK11 3LW, UK
UKHW022109190926
475702UK00013B/1350

* 9 7 8 1 1 3 8 9 8 4 0 3 5 *